In The Footsteps of Giants

Events and Personalities
From Calgary's Early History
For Young Readers

Chinook Country
Historical Society

We acknowledge the support of the Calgary Foundation and of ARC Resources Ltd. Through their generosity, we were able to bring this book to the youth of Alberta and to distribute, free of charge, copies to schools and libraries.

Library and Archives Canada Cataloguing in Publication
In the footsteps of giants : events and personalities from Calgary's early history for young readers.

ISBN 978-1-55383-412-0 (volume 1 : paperback)

1. Calgary (Alta.)—History—Juvenile literature. 2. Calgary (Alta.)— Biography—Juvenile literature. I. Chinook Country Historical Society, issuing body

FC3697.33.I58   2015 j971.23   C2015-906506-2

First printing, 2015
Second printing, 2017

Printed and bound in Canada by   Friesens Corporation
                                       History Book Division
                                       Altona MB R0G 0B0

Published by: Chinook Country Historical Society
                     # 311, 223 12 Ave SW
                     Calgary AB T2R 0G9

Table of Contents

Acknowledgements

In the Footsteps of Giants is Chinook Country Historical Society's first children's book project. It is a special commemorative project in recognition of the 25th annual Historic Calgary Week held July 23 to August 3, 2015. Producing books and anthologies is one of the ways that Chinook Country Historical Society achieves our objective "to promote a greater understanding of Canadian and Alberta history in Chinook Country for people of all ages."

Chinook Country Historical Society (CCHS) would like to acknowledge those that were instrumental in bringing this publication to fruition.

Firstly, the Children's Book Committee comprised of Walt and Irene DeBoni, Roberta Ryckman, Brenda Etherington, David Peyto, Rob Lennard, and Chairman David Finch spent many hours contacting authors, reading scripts and sourcing photographs and illustrations. The CCHS Board of Directors assumed board responsibilities for the project with Treasurer David Sztain managing the financial duties on the project.

CCHS extends a special 'thank you' to project authors – each volunteered many hours researching and writing their respective chapter and suggesting photographs to enhance the story.

The Historical Society of Alberta, with its long list of publications, is an incredible resource for its five local chapters. Debbie Goodine, Office Manager of the Historical Society of Alberta, provided much encouragement and assistance. Thank you.

Our appreciation is extended to Meaghan Craven whose editing expertise was instrumental in pulling together the disparate efforts of the authors into a coherent compilation.

Thanks also to Jim Beckel and Lynda Hiebert of Friesens Corporation, History Book Division, for believing in this project and then delivering a great product.

Thank you to Faye Reineberg Holt who generously donated a number of signed copies of her books to CCHS as a fundraiser for this children's book project.

And finally, the support of our sponsors was vital in bringing this exciting history to life. We would like to thank the Calgary Foundation and ARC Resources Ltd. for their generous financial contribution to our project.

Donna Zwicker, President
Chinook Country Historical Society

Introduction

Welcome to Calgary's exciting early history! It is full of interesting events and captivating, colourful and, dare we say, sometimes capricious characters that set the stage for the fabulous city we have today. Indeed, it was a difficult task to narrow down the list of people and events to include – there are so many. In fact, this is the first book and it will be followed by a second one next year. The individuals we have included are not always some of the most prominent in our history but are ones that often made a quiet but important contribution to the growth and vitality of the community.

The material is designed for children eight to twelve years of age and is written in a manner that will be interesting to them. It is not a historical novel even though there will be dialogue throughout the book. The historical facts, to the best of our knowledge, are accurate but depicted in a manner that makes for easier reading. At the end of each chapter we have included activity suggestions that offer an opportunity to further explore the history of the pioneers of our community.

In the book, you will meet our fictional Sarah, eleven years old, and her nine-year old brother Harry. Harry is in Grade four and his teacher has made the Social Studies curriculum come alive for the students. Harry is very excited about Alberta's history. Sarah had the same teacher two years ago and she too is very interested in history. During these classes, Sarah and Harry have learned about some of the major events and people that were important in building a strong Alberta.

Join Sarah and Harry as they experience Calgary and area today while learning more about the people and events of the past.

Many dinosaurs roamed the Bow Valley in prehistoric times.
Credit: Mural in the Royal Tyrell Museum. Photo by Walt DeBoni

When Dinosaurs and Sabretooths Roamed the Bow Valley

Cory W. Gross

Sarah and Harry loved Historic Calgary Week. Every summer at the end of July they bugged their parents to take them on all the different tours of the interesting places around Calgary they had never been before. Some were tours of cemeteries (Harry really liked those), others were trips to beautiful old buildings, and still others were chances to walk around in other communities to see homes that were seventy-five or a hundred years old or more. Sarah was particularly excited about today's tour. She loved science and nature, and this morning they were going to Nose Hill to learn about Calgary's prehistoric past.

After stopping briefly for morning coffee (for their parents) and hot chocolate (for Sarah and Harry), they arrived at the Sixty-Fourth Avenue parking lot at Nose Hill. The hill rose high above them, covered in prairie grasses, summer wildflowers, and tree-lined valleys. Sarah had already completed some research on Nose Hill at the library near their house and learned that it was over eleven square kilometres and the second largest park in Calgary, as well as one of the biggest urban parks in North America. She also learned that nobody really knows why it's called Nose Hill. That was the name that the first European settlers in the area learned from the First Nations.

The tour started, and they walked up the path to a cluster of sandstone boulders. The tour guide, Bill, hopped up on one of the boulders and started talking:

1

"65 million years ago, Calgary was very different from today. The world was much warmer, and we were almost on the coast of a vast inland sea that stretched from the Arctic Circle down to the Gulf of Mexico. Instead of dry prairie, this area was a lush, tropical swamp like what you would find today in Florida or Louisiana in the United States. Instead of bison, deer, and grizzly bears, we had Triceratops, duck-billed dinosaurs, and Tyrannosaurus rex. To the west, the Rocky Mountains were just starting to rise, and that was causing some very big changes for North America. As the mountains grew larger and the land rose higher, the inland sea started to drain away. As the sea drained away, the environment changed. Then a meteorite struck the Yucatan Peninsula in Mexico, killing off all the large dinosaurs, flying reptiles, marine reptiles, and many other living things.

"The rock I'm standing on is from the Paskapoo Formation. The word 'formation' is used by geologists to identify a layer of rock in the ground. It dates from 59 to 63 million years ago, so just after the big meteorite impact. This type of rock formed because of the rivers pouring out of the Rocky Mountains, carrying a lot of sand and silt with them. All this sand and silt was left behind in river channels and flood plains, and over time it was buried and squeezed and cemented together to become sandstone."

A glacier terminus as it enters the sea.
Credit: Walt DeBoni

2

Sarah remembered how many of the old buildings she saw on Historic Calgary Week tours were built out of the same yellow-grey sandstone rock. She also remembered seeing fossil clamshells in some of the buildings. It all made sense! If the rocks were made from rivers, then the rivers must have had clams.

"The most recent ice age began about two and a half million years ago," the guide continued. "Technically we are still in an ice age! An ice age is defined as a time when there is permanent ice at the North and South Poles."

Sarah raised her hand. "If we're still in an ice age, why is the climate getting warmer?"

"Good question! Our current ice age isn't the first one. About 850 million years ago, Earth was covered completely with ice and snow! By looking at the rocks left behind by past ice ages, we know that ice ages can last anywhere from 30 million to 300 million years. We also know that they are cyclical: they go through 50,000 to 100,000 year-long periods of where the glaciers grow very large (called a glacial period), and 10,000 to 40,000 year-long periods where they melt back (called an interglacial period). Right now we are living in an interglacial period that began about 13,000 years ago. We're due for the glaciers to start growing again. That's not what's happening though. Even though all the conditions in nature are right for it, the glaciers are shrinking and the ice caps at the poles are melting. That is why scientists have been looking at what human beings have been doing to see if all of our cars, factories, power plants, and things are having an effect on Earth's climate."

The tour continued on. Up the path they went, until the guide stopped them below a giant boulder sitting on the side of the hill. He began to tell them the story of this boulder as it is told by the Blackfoot First Nation.

"A long time ago on a very hot summer day, the old man Napi was out walking. Very tired from the heat, he found a nice big boulder, laid down his bison robe, and took a nap. As a thank you to the boulder, Napi left behind his bison robe. Unfortunately, the weather took a turn for the worse, and Napi got very cold. He went back to the boulder and asked for his robe back. 'No,' said the boulder, 'this was a gift, you can't just take it back.' Napi took the robe back anyway, thinking that there was nothing a mere boulder could do to stop him. 'Oh yeah?' the boulder said, and it started rolling after him! Napi ran off with the boulder chasing after him. Along the way Napi asked the different animals for help – the elk, the bison, the pronghorn, the bear – but none of them could stop the boulder. The best they could do was knock off little bits of it. Finally Napi asked the bats for help.

"'But we're so small! What can we do?' they asked. Napi didn't care!

"'Just do something!' he shouted.

The glacial erratic carried by an ancient glacier and left behind near Okotoks when the glacier melted.
Credit: Walt DeBoni

"The bats circled over the rolling boulder and decided to dive and hit it right in the middle. It cracked in half and stopped on the spot. That is why bats have smushed-in faces. The Blackfoot called the boulder 'Okotoks' (which means 'Big Rock'), and it can still be seen today south of Calgary, just outside the town of Okotoks. The boulder on Nose Hill is one of the pieces the other animals knocked off of it. This one is also called a 'bison rubbing rock' because bison came here to rub off their thick winter coats for thousands of years."

Sarah thought the story of Napi and Okotoks was a good one for telling people how to behave properly: don't give someone a gift and then try to take it back later. She was also curious about what scientists thought about the boulder.

"Bill," interjected Sarah, "how did the boulders get here?"

4

"When the glaciers began to grow in the mountains," the guide said, "rocks from the surrounding cliffs would fall on top of them. These rocks were carried out of the mountains by the glaciers, and when the glaciers melted, they just dropped the rocks in place. Geologists call these rocks 'glacial erratics,' and we can find them all over southern Alberta. There are some big ones here in Nose Hill, West Nose Creek Park, and Fish Creek Park, but the biggest one of all is Okotoks. Comparing the type of rock in these glacial erratics to rocks in the Rocky Mountains, geologists figured out that they originally came from Tonquin Valley, near Mount Edith Cavell in Jasper National Park. That's about six hundred kilometres away!"

Off they went again, climbing higher and higher up the hill. The path wound around a valley and a grove of trees. Soon they reached the very top. It was flatter up there than Sarah and Harry were expecting. Sarah remembered reading that the city used to dig up the gravel on the top of Nose Hill for use in roads and pathways.

Harry was the type of boy who looked down when he walked because he didn't want to trip on anything. It was a good thing he did, because he noticed a strange rock on the pathway. It wasn't very big, and it was round, but the strange thing was that it had what looked like little tubes running all through it. These were filled with a lighter coloured rock. Harry grabbed it and went running up to the guide to ask what it was. Bill was excited.

"Wow! You just found a fossil. These little things that look like tubes are actually an ancient coral named *Siphonodendron*. Usually you only find this in the mountains. This rock must have been carried by rivers or glaciers, and then left here on top of Nose Hill with the rest of the gravel. You have very good eyes!" Bill passed the rock around so that everyone could see the fossil.

The tour finally stopped at a group of boulders overlooking the whole city of Calgary. From where they were, Sarah and Harry could see downtown and its skyscrapers, little Nose Creek, Deerfoot Trail, and the airport. The wind rustled past them, carrying the scent of prairie flowers and grasses. The guide stretched out his arms and started talking.

"About 13,000 years ago, the glaciers began to melt. To the east would be

A view of downtown Calgary from Nose Hill.
Credit: Walt DeBoni

one great wall of ice: the Laurentide Ice Sheet coming down from the Arctic. To the west, another great wall of ice: the Cordilleran Ice Sheet coming down from the mountains. And in front of us, where Calgary sits today, would have been a huge glacial lake. Meltwater from the glaciers collected here, leaving behind a thick layer of silt. That is why Calgary looks like it has three layers. The top are hills like Nose Hill, and the bottom is the valley cut by the Bow and Elbow Rivers. In between is a plateau that was once the bottom of the glacial lake. Once the Laurentide Ice Sheet melted back far enough, the lake could drain away toward Hudson Bay.

"At this time, the plains of North America were like the great savannah of Africa, only colder. Many of the same kinds of animals lived here. We had elephant-like woolly mammoths, giant bison, giant sloths, and beavers the size of black bears. We had the sabre-toothed cat *Smilodon*, and lions and wolves, and the ferocious short-faced bear. We also had horses, which evolved in North America but went extinct at the same time as mammoths and *Smilodon*. The horses that run free in North America today are actually descendants of domesticated horses that were brought over from Europe by the Spanish. We also had some very familiar animals: Canada geese, whitetail deer, pronghorn antelopes, ducks, cougars, and black bears."

The woolly mammoth is an extinct prehistoric relative of today's Asian elephant. It was well adapted to the cold environment of the last ice age.
Credit: Adapted from image on commons.wikimedia.org by Author WolfmanSF

Bill told them about how pronghorn antelopes can run up to ninety kilometres an hour, which used to be a big mystery. Coyotes, the main predator of pronghorn antelopes today, can only run about seventy kilometres an hour. Scientists wondered why the pronghorn evolved to run so much faster than its main predator. But then they discovered the fossils of cheetahs that used to live in North America during the ice age. Cheetahs can also run up to ninety kilometres an hour. Pronghorns evolved to outrun cheetahs!

The cheetah is a modern "cousin" of the cheetahs that would have roamed the Bow Valley.
Credit: Walt DeBoni

While he was talking, the guide passed around an interesting collection of fossil teeth. After already finding a fossil, Harry was really excited about seeing more. The tooth from a baby woolly mammoth was the same size as his whole hand. It was big and covered in ridges, because mammoths ate tough grasses. Bill also passed around teeth from prehistoric horses and bison, and giant sloths. The coolest, Harry thought, was the tooth from a *Smilodon*. It was fifteen centimetres long and shaped like a dagger! The guide said that *Smilodon* would jump on its prey and hold it down, then use its teeth to bite into its neck, killing it.

"We also find evidence of First Nations in this area at the same time," he continued. "South of Calgary, at St. Mary's Reservoir, is a fantastic fossil site dating to 13,000 years ago. Trackways and fossils show woolly mammoths, camels, horses, bison, musk ox, and caribou. There is also evidence that First Nations peoples were hunting ancient horses and cutting them up to transport the meat back to their camps.

"Not far from here, in the community of Hawkwood, is another archaeological site dating to 8,250 years ago. At that site, there are spear tips and bison bones, but no bones from mammoths or horses. It took less than three thousand years for all those amazing animals to become extinct. What we see today – bears and deer and geese and moose – are the survivors."

"What made them go extinct?" asked Sarah.

"Usually it takes more than just one thing to drive a species into extinction," replied the guide. "When the glaciers began to melt, the environment started to change. The cold grasslands that the woolly mammoths liked were being slowly replaced by forest. All those melting glaciers also raised the sea level by several metres, flooding the land that mammoths lived on. So mammoths weren't doing very well already. Then along came human hunters who might have overhunted mammoths into extinction. The same thing might have happened to giant sloths and giant bison and prehistoric horses. Without their prey, predators like *Smilodon* and lions would have gone extinct, too.

"Unfortunately we see the same sort of thing happening today. As cities and farms grow, people alter the natural environment, making it harder for the animals that live there to survive. It's even worse when people hunt the animals. Some scientists say that the extinction event that killed off the mammoths and sabretooths never actually stopped. Did you know that about

8

30,000 elephants are illegally killed each year so that poachers can steal their ivory tusks? Or that grizzly bears used to live all over western North America, but are now reduced almost completely to British Columbia, the Yukon, and Alaska? Bison almost did go extinct until people recognized that we needed to protect them and their habitat so the species could survive. It is estimated that by 1894, there were only twenty-five Plains Bison in the wild. Today there are 15,000 roaming in the wild and over 500,000 in reserves and ranches."

Sarah felt sorry for elephants and grizzly bears, but she was excited about how the bison was saved from extinction. As she looked out over the grassy top of Nose Hill on their way back to their car, she started to wonder about

A woolly mammoth skeleton at the Royal Tyrell Museum.
Credit: Display at the Royal Tyrell Museum. Photo by Walt DeBoni

what she could do to help the living relatives of all those amazing ice-age animals today.

Activities

1. Take your own tour of Nose Hill. Everything that Sarah and Harry saw on their tour is real, and you can see it for yourself. Begin at Sixty-Fourth Avenue parking lot and follow the path up the hill (the valley full of bushes and trees should be to your left). You will pass the cluster of Paskapoo sandstone rocks and the large glacial erratic. The path will take you south (left) around the valley full of trees and up to the flat top of Nose Hill, which used to be a gravel quarry. Continue to follow the path left until you reach the group of boulders that give you a good look over the entire city. Bring a camera to take pictures, and a sketchbook to draw what you see and write notes. Look closely at colours, textures, and differences in the types of rocks. Keep your eyes peeled for fossils. Be a nature explorer! **Remember**: please leave what you find in the park for others to enjoy, including the rocks and the flowers.

2. Drive down to the town of Okotoks to see the Big Rock that chased Napi. Make sure your parents look it up before you go, so you know where you're heading. Signs at the boulder give you more information and a more detailed version of the Blackfoot story. Read it aloud. If you go with friends or siblings, you may even want to act the story out. There is lots of room at the site to run around and play Napi and the Big Rock.

3. Be an urban fossil hunter. Whenever you see a building made out of yellow-grey sandstone, stop and take a good look at it. See if you can find any fossils. Paskapoo sandstone is well-known for having fossilized clams and oysters, petrified wood, and very rarely insects and mammal tracks. If you would like to see a really good example, visit Edworthy Park. Right in front of the bridge at the Memorial Drive entrance are some boulders full of oyster-shell fossils.

4. Learn about an endangered animal. It could be one from far away, or one from right here in Alberta. Find out about how it lives and what

kind of environment it lives in. Educate yourself on why that animal has become endangered and what you might be able to do to help it survive. It could be anything from being careful about what you buy when grocery shopping to helping raise money for conservation.

5. Which is the largest park in Calgary? How does that park differ from Nose Hill Park?

Further Reading

Huck, Barbara, and Doug Whiteway. *In Search of Ancient Alberta.* Winnipeg: Heartland Publications, 1998.

Royal Tyrrell Museum of Palaeontology. *The Land Before Us: The Making of Ancient Alberta.* Edmonton: Lone Pine Publishing, 1994.

Royal Tyrrell Museum and Monique Keiran. *Reading the Rock: A Biography of Ancient Alberta.* Calgary: Red Deer Press, 2004.

This is a stylized photograph of the Livingston house at Heritage Park. It is one-half of the original Livingston house in Glenmore. The house was built with a log wall down the middle and with a staircase on each side. Upstairs on one side were the boys' bedrooms and on the other side were the girls' bedrooms. The other half of the house was separated and sold before this portion was moved to Heritage Park.
Credit: Walt DeBoni

Sam and Jane Livingston, Pioneers

Walt DeBoni

It was after 8:00 pm, and Sarah and Harry had just gone to bed, although they were not ready to go to sleep yet. Their mother had just turned out the light in each of their bedrooms after kissing them both good night with the advice that they should go to sleep, as tomorrow was another busy day at school.

Harry was just bursting to tell Sarah about the exciting day he had had in school that day, when their teacher talked to the class about some of the pioneers in early Alberta history. He walked softly into Sarah's room to talk to her. "There was this guy, Sam Livingston, who was a gold prospector, trader, and farmer who travelled all over North America and finally settled in Calgary. And his wife, Jane, must have been an amazing woman as she had fourteen children. Can you imagine having thirteen brothers and sisters?" Harry exclaimed.

"Wow, I'd sure like to meet Sam and Jane," said Sarah. "They must have been quite the parents!"

Harry walked back to his bedroom and eventually, fell asleep, and it wasn't long before he started dreaming. He found himself in a rustic home with an elderly lady dressed in what looked like a costume from Heritage Park.

"Hello, young man, how are you?" she said.

Harry, somewhat startled, stammered, "I'm f-f-fine, thank you." And then he noticed a different-looking wedding ring on her finger.

The lady saw him looking at her ring finger and said, "My husband, Sam Livingston, had this ring made for me, and I got it only after he died. Look, it says 'In Memory Of...' on it. I treasure this ring. It stands for our love for each other and the many years we spent together in the pioneer days of western Canada."

"At school, we've been studying the early days of the European settlers in western Canada. Can you tell me more about your life?" said Harry.

"Of course, I can. Perhaps I should start with the life of my

A photograph of Jane Livingston, about 1898-99, taken shortly after Sam died.
Credit: Glenbow Archives NA-1494-3

grandfather, Joseph Howse, who came to Canada from England in about 1795. Western Canada was known as Rupert's Land then, and Grandfather worked for the Hudson's Bay Company, first in a place called York Factory that was an important settlement on Hudson Bay, involved in fur trading. Later, in about 1810, Grandfather went west and established the first Hudson's Bay Company post west of the Rocky Mountains. He had married a Cree lady, Mary, and I believe they had only two children, one of whom was my father Henry Howse. My mother was Janet Spence."

"My grandmother was a remarkable woman. Even after marrying my grandfather, she raised her family almost by herself since Grandfather was away most of the time exploring western Canada. And in 1815, Grandfather returned to England, leaving Grandmother in Canada."

"What was your life like when you were a child?" asked Harry.

"I had twelve brothers and sisters, although two of them died at a very young age before I was born. That happened quite often, as there was very little medicine at the time and very few doctors. We lived in a one-room house so, you can imagine, we were quite crowded."

Harry couldn't help interrupting her.

The interior of the Livingston house in Heritage Park with a lady dressed up as Jane Livingston.
Credit: Walt DeBoni

"Wow, my sister and I each have our own bedroom. I can't imagine all those people eating and sleeping in one room."

Jane smiled and continued, "The buffalo, what you now call bison, was a very important source of food, and every year the men and women went on buffalo hunts. After the men killed the buffalo, it was the women's job to cut up the meat, clean and prepare the hides, dry the meat over smoky fires, and make the pemmican – that's a mixture of dried meat, fat, and dried berries – that we ate in the winter when we couldn't hunt the buffalo. Also, we sold some of the pemmican at the fur-trading posts, since the fur traders carried the pemmican for food while they travelled in the wilderness. We could use the money to buy other goods from the trading post."

In his dream, Harry interrupted again. "How did your parents look after so many children? That must have been really hard."

"All the children were expected to help as much as they could," Jane said, "and by the time I was fifteen or sixteen, I was expected to work as hard as my parents. We helped picking berries and other things that grew around us, and also we would catch small animals or birds to help feed the family.

"By the time I was sixteen, the buffalo became scarce, and more people from eastern Canada were moving into the area where we lived, so my parents decided to move farther west. In 1864 we set out in Red River oxcarts, and after several weeks going across the prairies we settled on the North Saskatchewan River at Fort Victoria. These Red River carts were quite the contraptions, all made of wood, not like the fancy metal cars that you have today. They had big wooden wheels and a small tree trunk served as an axle to connect them. You can imagine the noise when the wheels turned, even though we put grease on the axles. It's a wonder I didn't lose my hearing!"

"I thought Victoria was on Vancouver Island," interjected Harry.

"That's a different place. Several places were named for the queen of England at the time, Queen Victoria. Fort Victoria was a fur-trading post set up east of Edmonton by George Flett for the Hudson's Bay Company. My father had worked for the company before, and he was able to work for them again. Also at the post was a Reverend George McDougall, who had set up a Methodist mission to work with the Natives in the region.

"And, it was here that I met Sam Livingston. We were married in 1865, and I was only seventeen! Back then, it was quite usual to be married at a young age. We were married at the Hudson's Bay post. Sam had a remarkable life, and I will have to tell you more about him at another time."

"Gee, my aunt and uncle were almost thirty when they got married," said Harry.

Jane smiled again, and continued her story.

"The first three of our fourteen children, Jane, Nellie, and George, were born while we lived at Fort Victoria. We moved south to what is now Calgary in 1873 and eventually established a farm on the Elbow River, south of the

16

new North West Mounted Police Fort Calgary. It was here that for the first time in my life I lived in a house with more than one room! Sam and I built a large log house for our growing family."

Sam and Jane Livingston's house on its original location in Glenmore. The small cabin in the right side of the picture was the original home on the farm while they built the larger house.
Credit: Glenbow Archives NA-126-1

"Gee, that sounds very interesting," said Harry. "Can I come talk to you again, sometime?"

"Of course you can, young man," said Jane.

And then, Harry woke up to see that it was morning, and Sarah was just coming into his room.

"You wouldn't believe what a dream I had last night! I was listening to Jane Livingston telling me about her life," said Harry. "I can't wait to tell you her story!"

"That's amazing," said Sarah. "I dreamed that I was travelling with Sam Livingston on his journey from Ireland to the California gold fields and eventually to western Canada."

"Sounds like a great dream! Why did Sam leave Ireland?" asked Harry.

"Well, I dreamed that he left in 1848 when he was only sixteen years old, at a time when Ireland was in the midst of a potato famine. The Irish people depended on potatoes for their food, and when there were several crop failures because of a potato disease, called 'blight,' more than one million Irish people died from starvation and disease. About another million people left the country, with many of them coming to Canada and the United States," said Sarah.

"Sam travelled to California, which was in the middle of a gold rush. He had dreams of striking it rich and returning to Ireland to buy some land. He didn't find a lot of gold, but he was bitten by the gold bug. He just had to find gold, so he carried on to look for gold in the northwestern United States," said Sarah.

"When did he come to Canada, then?" asked Harry.

Sam Livingston with his flowing beard and his leather jacket with fringes. Photo taken about 1890.
Credit: Glenbow Archives NA-94-1

"I'm not exactly sure when, but in the early 1860s he was panning for gold in British Columbia, again without huge success, when his friend Jim Gibbons told him about panning for gold on the North Saskatchewan River near Fort Edmonton. The gold found near Fort Edmonton apparently was very fine and difficult to separate from the other soil. Still, Sam figured that he would find some way of panning the gold, so he and fourteen other gold bugs set off for Fort Edmonton.

"The only problem was that they didn't really know how to get to Fort Edmonton or the North Saskatchewan River. They travelled east through the Rocky Mountains through the Kicking Horse Pass."

"Were there lots of horses up there or something?" Harry asked.

"No, Harry. The first European explorers to walk through this pass were led by Captain John Palliser in 1858. It's called the Kicking Horse because

James Hector, one of the explorers, was kicked by his horse while in the pass.

"Anyway, after the group of gold seekers wandered around for a while, coming across several rivers but not the North Saskatchewan, they split up into three groups. Sam Livingston and Jim Gibbons travelled north and wandered the countryside looking for the river. At one point in the fall, they lost their last horse to a raiding party of Blackfoot people. They were tired and hungry, but they pressed on and followed a trail in the snow. Lucky for them, they stumbled into the Hudson's Bay Company post at Rocky Mountain House. There were only a few people there, including a Catholic missionary Father Lacombe."

"Hey, learned about him in school!" Harry exclaimed.

"Yes. Father Lacombe helped Sam and Jim, feeding them and giving them a place to sleep. After resting up for a few days, they were provided with snowshoes and directions to Fort Edmonton by the people at Rocky Mountain House. They finally got to Fort Edmonton and then decided that they would rather go a little farther downstream to Fort Victoria. It was here that Sam met his future wife, Jane Howse," said Sarah.

"Yes," exclaimed Harry. "They married in 1865, and a few years later they moved south and settled near Calgary."

The first threshing machine in the Calgary area on Sam Livingston's farm about 1886-1889.
Credit: Glenbow Archives NA-1494-49

"That's right, Harry," said Sarah. "When Sam and Jane first moved to Calgary with their four children in the early 1870s, he worked mostly as a trader. In 1875 he was getting ready to build a home where Fort Calgary is today. When the North West Mounted Police arrived, he decided to move up the Elbow River. Then in about 1876, he established a farm on the Elbow River, in the area we now know as the Glenmore Reservoir. It was here that he and Jane built their log house, and that house now sits in Heritage Park.

"Apparently a teacher lived with them in their house and educated their children," said Sarah.

"I'm not sure I would like that," Harry commented.

"Sam was an innovative farmer, bringing some farm equipment to the West and successfully growing grain, raising cattle, and planting fruit trees that he imported into the area. He was also involved with the Calgary District Agricultural Society, and in 1884 went to Toronto where the society showed off grains and other produce at the Industrial Exhibition to promote immigration to the Calgary region," said Sarah.

"He must have been quite an interesting individual," Harry piped up. "I remember seeing a statue of him at the Calgary Airport. It looks like he had a big beard, long hair, and wore a buckskin jacket and

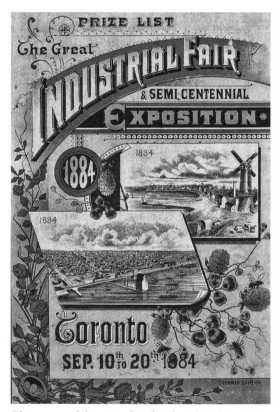

The cover of the prize list for the 1884 Exposition that Sam Livingston attended and displayed agricultural products from the Calgary area.
Credit: City of Toronto Archives, Fonds 70, Series 756, File 3

20

wide-brimmed hat. I'll bet that when he walked into a room, people sat up and took notice of him."

Activities

1. Visit the Livingston home at Heritage Park in Calgary.
   a. Is the home in Heritage Park as large as the original Livingston house?
   b. Why was the house moved?
2. Sam Livingston has been called Calgary's first citizen by some, but others have also been given that title. Do an Internet search and decide for yourself who best deserves the title of Calgary's first citizen.
3. Where does the name "Glenmore" come from?
4. Can you find on a map Avoca, Ireland, the town where Sam Livingston was born?

Further Reading

Jameson, Sheilagh S. "Livingston, Samuel Henry Harkwood." *The Dictionary of Canadian Biography*. Accessed May 9, 2015. http://www.biographi. ca/en/bio/livingston_samuel_henry_harkwood_12E.html.

Hancock, Lyn, and Marion Dowler. *The Ring: Memories of a Metis Grandmother*. Lantzville, BC: Lyn Hancock Books, 2010.

MacEwan, Grant. *Fifty Mighty Men*. Vancouver, BC: Greystone Books, 1995. (The Local History Room at the Central Library has an earlier edition of this book, located at: J971.2MACE.)

Chumek, S., and N. Kenneth. *The Spirit of Alberta: An Illustrated Heritage*. Edmonton: Alberta Heritage Foundation, 1978. (This book doesn't include Sam Livingston, but it is a good source of information about Alberta pioneers. You can find it at the library under 971.23SPI)

Artwork by Richard Barrington Nevitt of the North West Mounted Police. Image of the Methodis
Mission, Morleyville, 1875.
Credit: Glenbow Archives NA-51-2

Reverend George McDougall

Kate Reeves

It was a summer Sunday afternoon, and Sarah and her brother Harry were returning from a weekend at Banff. Their father had decided to take the slower, more scenic route back to Calgary, along Highway 1A on the north side of the Bow River. This was the old highway, before the TransCanada Highway was built. They were more than halfway home when Sarah spotted a sign by the side of the road that said "Historic Site Open" and asked her father to stop.

"What is an historic site?" asked Harry.

McDougall United Church, 2012.
Credit: Walt DeBoni

"It is where something important happened in the past," his father replied.

"I don't see anything but a church," thought Harry. "What could be important about that?"

Their father parked the car by the road near a monument made of rocks. Sarah wanted to read what was on the monument, but Harry was already running down the path to the church. When Sarah caught up to him, he was tugging at the front door, but it was locked.

"I thought it was supposed to be open!" he said.

"Look," said Sarah, "this must be a graveyard." Next to the church was a gravestone. They read the words written on it:

Sacred to the Memory of
Rev. George McDougall
Aged 54 Years

The deceased was for 16 years
Chairman of the Weslyan Missions in the North-West.
He lost his way on the prairie
about 40 miles east of this place
on January 24th 1876.
His body was found on the 5th
of the following month
and interred here by his
sorrowing family who have
erected this tribute to his memory.

"What does 'interred' mean?" asked Harry.

"I think it means buried," answered Sarah.

Just then a woman appeared from behind the church. She had a name tag that said DOCENT.

"Is Docent your name?" asked Harry.

"No," smiled the woman. "My name is Laura. A docent is a volunteer who acts as a guide. I'm here to answer your questions."

"Oh," said Sarah. "My name is Sarah and this is my brother Harry."

"Is someone buried there?" asked Harry.

"The monument is a bit misleading," said Laura. "Reverend George McDougall did die after a buffalo hunt in 1876, but he is buried in the Stoney Cemetery across the road and up the hill. The headstone was moved here so visitors like you could read it. There is another monument where they found Reverend McDougall's body. It used to be outside of Calgary, near Balzac, but because the city has grown so much, it is now inside the city."

"We have gone to a big building downtown in Calgary called the McDougall Centre. Well, at least in the garden outside the building. They had a Stampede breakfast there. Was that named after George McDougall?" asked Sarah.

"Yes, that's right," said Laura. "And there is a mountain named after him in the Kananaskis."

"Wow," said Harry. "A mountain. What did he do that was so important?"

"Yes," said Sarah. "Who was George McDougall?"

"He was a Methodist missionary. Methodism is a Christian church, but you don't hear about it anymore because it became part of the United Church of Canada in 1925. But back in the 1800s, when George was young,

The sign at the entrance to McDougall Church showing some of the syllabics alphabet created by one of the missionaries.
Credit: Walt DeBoni

the Methodists thought education was very important. They wanted to help educate the Native people, thinking that would help them have a good life when the buffalo were gone. Methodists also wanted Native peoples to be able to read the Bible. Because the First Nations in this area, the Cree, didn't have a system of writing, one of the missionaries created an alphabet. It is called syllabics. It is on the sign at the beginning of the path."

"I saw it!" said Sarah. "It looks like triangles and squiggles."

"If you want to come inside the church with your parents, I can tell you more about George McDougall and his family and show you a Bible written in Cree syllabics," said Laura.

"But the door is locked," said Harry.

"That is the bell tower entrance, not the church entrance," replied Laura. "The bell tower was added later, after the McDougalls moved to Calgary. Come around to the back and you will see the entrance."

When Sarah and Harry went inside the church, the first thing they saw was a potbellied stove in the middle of the aisle. "That is a funny place to put it," said Harry. "Everyone has to go around it."

The potbellied stove in the McDougall Church.
Credit: Walt DeBoni

"That is true," said Laura, "but the stove was needed in the winter. There is still no electricity or heating in this building. Putting the stove in the middle of the room made it easier to heat the whole room."

"Why is there a round circle but no window on that wall?" asked Sarah.

"My, you are quite observant!" said Laura. "Perhaps the McDougalls intended to put a stained-glass window in that wall, but they never did." On either side of the circle was

26

One of two paintings inside McDougall Church showing the McDougall's trip west.
Credit: Walt DeBoni

27

a large painting. The pictures in the painting told the story of the McDougalls' journey west. "George McDougall and his wife Elizabeth, were working with the Native people in Ontario and Manitoba," Laura explained, "when George was made the superintendent of the western missions. This was before Canada was Canada. Back then, this part of the country was known to Europeans and white settlers as Rupert's Land. The McDougalls started a mission east of Edmonton, but in 1870 there was a smallpox epidemic. Three of their daughters died, as well as their son's wife, Abigail."

"That's sad," said Sarah.

"Yes," said Laura. "Their son became a missionary, too. His name was John. There is a picture of him and his second wife, Elizabeth, here on the wall. John and his father George picked this spot for a mission to the Stoney people. The other couple is another brother, David, and his wife, Annie. David was a free trader. That means he worked for himself and not the Hudson's Bay Company. His store was just across the creek."

"May I go up to the balcony?" asked Harry.

"Yes, let's go, but be careful. The floor is sloped."

When they were in the balcony, Laura pointed out the marks on the wood that showed that the wood had been cut with a whipsaw. "You would need two men to use that kind of blade," she said.

"Did they have help building the church?" asked Sarah.

"Yes, Andrew Sibbald came with them. He had been a carpenter, but he lost his right hand in an accident so he studied to become a school teacher. He came to be a

Reverend John McDougall and his family, about 1886-94. L to R. Rev. John McDougall holding Morley, Mrs. John McDougall (nee Elizabeth Boyd), Mrs. George McDougall.
Credit: Glenbow Archives NA-1030-33

28

teacher in the mission, but he was still able to help with the building. In fact, he brought the pieces of a sawmill in his wagon when he came. That was before roads and trains. And there was also a Métis family, the Inksters, who were a great help to the McDougalls. Do you know what Métis means?"

"I know," said Sarah. "That means they were both Native and French."

"Yes, that is partly correct," answered Laura, "other Métis people are of Native and Scottish or other European heritage."

"Eventually some of the McDougalls' friends from the east came," said Laura. "They each built a house on a river lot. There were ten river lots from here to the Ghost River. Do you know what river lots are?"

"I think I know," said Sarah. "Instead of having your house on a square piece of land, it is on a long piece that goes to a river. Is that right?"

"Correct," said Laura. "The ten lots formed a community called Morleyville Settlement."

"Where did the Native people sleep?" asked Harry.

"The Stoney people had tipis; these were tents they could put up and take down easily when they moved to follow the buffalo." replied Laura. "But after the buffalo were gone, they built houses on their reserve. The reserve is all around us. A reserve is land that is 'reserved' for Native people. This was all decided at the signing of a treaty."

"We learned about that in school," said Sarah. "The treaty for this area is called Treaty 7."

"Yes," said Laura. "The missionaries advised the Natives to sign the treaty. They thought it would help them get schools and learn to farm."

"Did it?" asked Harry.

"Well, no. We know now that the schools were actually harmful for many of Canada's First Nations, and the land here was not good for farming. The problem was that settlers, missionaries, and the government were not respectful of the First Peoples' own wisdom. They were here for a long time before the non-Natives came. That is why they are called First Nations," said Laura.

"Our teacher says we are all Treaty People," said Sarah.

"I am glad to hear that, Sarah," replied Laura. "That means that we need to

29

First Nations and Reverend John McDougall (on right) at the 1912 Calgary Stampede.
Credit: Glenbow Archives NA-274-6

learn to listen to Native people so we can live in peace, friendship, and respect.

"Would you like to see where the McDougalls and their friends built a house and a barn and corral for the horses? Andrew Sibbald's house was here, too. I can show you where they were. We can see the cellar walls of the mission house."

Sarah and Harry's mom and dad said they could go, and so they followed Laura on a path that led away from the church toward the river. "Is that the Bow River?" asked Sarah.

"Yes, it is. Before there were bridges, the Native people used to cross the river here. That might be one of the reasons George McDougall picked this spot for the mission."

The path lead through some trees and stopped where there was a rectangle of crumbling cement in the ground. "But there are trees growing in the middle of it!" exclaimed Harry.

"Well, the house has been gone for a long time now. The buildings were used until 1921 and then a new church was built across the river in Morley. The train tracks were on that side, too, so eventually all the buildings were abandoned. They knocked them all down, but for some reason they left the church standing."

"I wonder why they didn't knock it down," thought Harry. "If no one was using it anymore."

"Can I look out over the cliff?" asked Harry.

"Okay," said Laura. "I'll go with you and show you where Andrew Sibbald's house was. His house was at the edge of the church property next to an embankment by the creek. The creek is named Jacob's Creek after a Stoney chief." said Laura. "We think Andrew Sibbald set up his sawmill somewhere along the creek."

"It is an awfully small creek," said Harry.

"That's true," said Laura. "It must have been bigger then. On the other side of the creek was David McDougall's store. He had to go down to Fort Benton in Montana to get supplies before the railway came through here in 1883. At one time there were more people getting their mail at David McDougall's store than at Fort Calgary. The North West Mounted Police built a post near there, too."

Laura led them back through the trees and showed them where wagon wheels had made ruts in the ground.

"Wow, neat!" said Harry. "This might be the oldest road in all of Alberta!"

"Well, maybe in this part of Alberta," said Laura.

The McDougalls would have used the British ensign flag, like this one, since Canada did not have its own flag at that time.
Credit: Walt DeBoni

When they got back to the church, the wind had come up. The flags made noises as their clips banged against the metal flagpole. "Why is that funny flag flying, instead of the usual maple leaf flag?" asked Harry.

"When the McDougalls came, there was no Canadian flag, and they used the British Ensign flag. We wanted it to look the way it did when they were here, so that is why we use that flag instead."

"I have one last question," said Harry. "Do you ever ring the bell in the bell tower?"

"Why, yes, we do," answered Laura. "When we have church services twice a year or for a wedding."

"Oh," said Harry, looking rather disappointed.

"And sometimes," said Laura, "just for the heck of it. Would you like to ring the bell?"

"Yes, please!" said Harry. Laura unlocked the door, and Harry and Sarah took turns pulling on the rope attached to the bell in the tower.

Afterward, their parents thanked Laura for answering all their questions. "You're welcome. Thank you for visiting us," said Laura.

As they drove away, Sarah thanked her father for stopping at the historic site. Harry, looked back at the church. "I know why they didn't knock the church down," he thought. "Something important happened there."

Activities

1. Visit the historic site on Highway 1A during the tourist season and ask to ring the bell.
2. Look up the syllabic alphabet and try to write your name using it.
3. Draw a picture of the British Ensign flag. Make sure it is right side up.
4. Ask permission to visit the cemetery across the road from the church. What names from Morleyville can you find?
5. Visit the Whyte Museum in Banff and find the exhibits on the McDougalls. Visit the Luxton Museum in Banff to see exhibits on the Stoney people's way of life.
6. Try and locate as many places as you can with the name McDougall. Which ones were named for the missionary family? (Hint: there are some in Airdrie, Calgary, Edmonton, Kananaskis, Morley, Pigeon Lake, Smokey Lake, Sundre, and Victoria Settlement.)
7. See if you can find the cairn that marks where Reverend George McDougall's body was found in 1876. (Hint: It is in Panorama Hills in Calgary's northwest.) Have a picnic there and try to imagine the

spot being part of a long ride on a horse from Fort Calgary.

8. Visit the Blackfoot Gallery at Glenbow Museum. You can read what the Blackfoot people think of the missionaries and the treaties and hear their voices in English and Blackfoot on special telephones.

9. Look up Blackfoot Crossing on a map of Alberta. Ask your parents if you can visit the Interpretive Centre there. You will hear Blackfoot stories from the past and present.

10. On pages 38 and 39 of *Reading Between the Lines: Piecing Together the Life of Elizabeth Boyd McDougall* by Shirley A. Serviss, read the six stories that relate the same event when one or more Native people appeared at the McDougall home while only the women were there. Discuss why the stories are different. What do you think really happened?

Further Reading

Serviss, Shirley A. *Reading Between the Lines: Piecing Together the Life of Elizabeth Boyd McDougall*. Edmonton: Rowan Books, 2000. (Using her imagination and building on extensive research, Serviss writes poetry portraying the life of Elizabeth Boyd McDougall. Note this book is available in the Local History Reading Room at Calgary's Central Library.)

There are not many books that are appropriate further reading on the McDougalls for young readers, but Shirley Serviss recommends a lot of books for older readers. A few of these books include:

Hungy Wolf, Adolf, and Beverly Hungry Wolf. *Indian Tribes of the Northern Rockies*. Skookumchuck, BC: Good Medicine Books, 1989.

MacEwan, Grant. *...and Mighty Women Too*. Saskatoon: Western Producer Prairie Books, 1975.

MacEwan, Grant. *Between the Red and the Rockies*. Toronto: University of Toronto Press, 1952.

McDougall, John. *In the Days of the Red River Rebellion*. Edmonton: University of Alberta Press, 1983.

McDougall, John. *Parsons on the Plains*. Edited by Thomas Bredin. Don Mills, ON: Longman Canada Limited, 1971.

Artwork by William Winder, about 1876. View at Fort Calgary. The Bow River is behind the fort and women are washing clothes in front of the cabin.
Credit: Glenbow Archives NA-98-3

The Arrival of the North West Mounted Police

Joan Lawrence

Learning about the archaeological sites and geology around Calgary during their trip to Nose Hill had made Sarah curious about how there came to be a city here. Historic Calgary Week was over and school wouldn't start for another few weeks. She didn't want to wait until then. She asked Mom where they could go to learn more.

"We could go to Fort Calgary," said Mom. "It's a National Historic Site. I'm sure they would be able to tell us about how the city started."

Harry and Dad agreed, so they decided to spend the next day at the Fort.

The morning was a perfect August day: warm and sunny, with a little bit of a breeze. The family drove down Macleod Trail toward downtown, then turned right onto Ninth Avenue SE. Just before they reached the bridge into Inglewood, they turned north into the parking lot of Fort Calgary.

Harry, Sarah, Mom and Dad went into the interpretive centre. The woman at the desk took their admission and handed them a brochure with a map of the site. "What brings you here today?" she asked.

Sarah was happy to tell her. "We want to learn more about how Calgary began," she said.

"Well," said the woman at the desk. "I'm sure Duncan would be happy to tell you. He's one of our guides." She waved to a young man wearing a nametag who was standing by the window. "Duncan, can you tell this family about Fort Calgary and the start of the city?"

"I sure can!" said Duncan, walking over to them. "What do you want to know?"

Harry spoke up. "Well, for starters, why is this called Fort Calgary? I don't see any fort!"

Duncan laughed. "How about we go outside and see?" he suggested. The family agreed, so he led them out of the interpretive centre and up a small hill. A large square area was outlined with red light and vertical shapes. As they got closer, they could see that the shapes were wooden figures. They walked into the middle of the square.

View of Fort Calgary, looking north, August 1881.
Credit: Glenbow Archives NA-235-2

"This is the parade square," said Duncan. "Right here is where the original Fort Calgary stood." He showed them a picture of Fort Calgary from 1881. A small wooden fort was surrounded by open prairie.

"Wow," said Dad, looking from the photo to the skyscrapers downtown. "Calgary has really grown!"

"It really has," Duncan agreed. He went on to explain that the Mounties chose this spot because this is where the rivers meet. This is also an important place in the traditional territory of the Blackfoot Confederacy. The Blackfoot Confederacy includes the Siksika, Piikani, and Kainaiwa Nations. All of these Nations have a lot in common, and they also each have their own unique heritage. Traditional Blackfoot territory stretches from south of the Montana border all the way north to Edmonton.

Non-Blackfoot Nations used the area around Calgary, too, including the Stoney Nakoda and the Tsuut'ina. The Cree sometimes came here to hunt, and there were several big battles between them and the Blackfoot. The Ktunaxa, or Kootenay, came here to trade from their territory west of the Rocky Mountains.

"For thousands of years, Indigenous people have lived in this area, and they are still here today," said Duncan. "But on July first, 1867, something happened that brought big changes. Can you think what that might have been?"

Harry knew what July first was. "Canada Day! Last year we came to a big celebration here at Fort Calgary."

"That's right: Canada Day, known as Dominion Day prior to 1982, marks the anniversary of Confederation. That is when the provinces of New Brunswick, Nova Scotia, Ontario and Quebec joined together, to create Canada. Manitoba and the Northwest Territories became part of Canada in 1870. British Columbia agreed to join in 1871, but only if the government built a railroad across the prairies. Canada's first prime minister, Sir John A. Macdonald, knew that he would have to make agreements with the people living on the prairies before the railroad could be built.

In the meantime, independent traders started to come into this area and set up trading posts. They collected thousands of buffalo robes, but many of them offered only whiskey in return. That caused a lot of problems. Another problem was that most of the traders were American, and the Canadian government was worried that the United States might want the Northwest Territories to become part of their country.

In 1873 the Government of Canada created the North West Mounted Police and sent them west the next summer to enforce Canadian law. There were only 275 men to patrol an area the size of western Europe! The first winter the Mounties split up. Some went to Fort Edmonton and spent the winter with the Hudson's Bay Company. Others went south and built Fort

Macleod. Another part of the Force travelled back to Swan River in Manitoba until spring arrived. They spent the summer of 1875 building more forts so they could patrol the area more efficiently. That is when they came here, to the confluence of the Bow and Elbow Rivers."

"What does confluence mean?" asked Harry.

"A place where things come together," explained Duncan. "At Fort Calgary, it is the place where the Elbow River joins the Bow River, but it is also where many different cultures come together. The red lights around us show the outline of the original Fort. Have a look at the upright shapes: what do they remind you of?"

Sarah looked more closely. "Oh! They're people!"

"That's right," said Duncan. "Remember when you asked where the fort was?" Harry nodded.

"Well," continued Duncan, "we decided not to try to recreate a fort that only lasted a few years. Instead, this exhibit represents all the people who make Calgary. That includes the people who were here when Calgary began, and all the people who came later and are here now. It is a place to reflect on the past, and on your own story as a Calgarian."

Fort Calgary, about 1878-79.
Credit: Glenbow Archives NA-5501-9

Duncan asked them to imagine what it might have been like before there was a city here. They stood for a moment and listened to the sound of the wind. They watched a group of Richardson's ground squirrels scurrying through the tall grass, and admired the blue water against the green willows on the riverbank.

"What a beautiful place to be," said Mom. "I can see why they chose it."

Dad said, "I heard that 'Calgary' means 'clear running water' in Gaelic. Is that true?"

"Not exactly," said Duncan. "Colonel Macleod was a high-ranking officer in the North West Mounted Police —"

"Oh, is that where Macleod Trail comes from?" interrupted Harry. Sarah scowled at him, but she was secretly glad he had asked, because she had wondered that too.

"That's right," said Duncan. "He was from the Isle of Mull in Scotland, and he remembered a place there called that. He thought it meant clear running water, but it actually means something closer to 'bay farm.' You can see why he thought it would be a good name, though, can't you?"

He told them that Calgary was not the first name for this spot. The Blackfoot had already called it *Moh'kinsstis*, or 'Elbow' because of the bend in the river. The Tsuut'ina called it *Kootsisáw*, and the Stoney Nakoda called it *Wincheesh-pah*, which mean 'Elbow' in their languages. For a little while, the Fort was called Fort Brisebois. Many of the forts were named for their commanding officers. Unfortunately for him, Inspector Brisebois was not popular with his men, so Colonel Macleod decided to change the name to Fort Calgary.

"Why didn't the men like him?" asked Harry.

"Life wasn't easy that first winter," replied Duncan. "The Fort was built by the I.G. Baker Company. They dug trenches and put upright logs in the trenches to make the walls. The holes between the logs were filled with mud, but it still wasn't very warm. Some men even slept in the riverbank, because it was warmer. The weather was extremely cold, and the men did not want to stay at their posts. Brisebois was not very good at keeping discipline, so

Muddy ground at the blacksmith shop, Fort Calgary, 1883.
Credit: Glenbow Archives NA-448-4

the men didn't like him. It didn't help that Brisebois had a stove to keep him warm, while the men only had a fireplace!"

Duncan showed them a picture of the 1875 Fort. Mud was everywhere! He explained that the roof leaked and it wasn't very comfortable. However, life was not all bad. The Fort soon became the centre of the community. Settlers and traders came to the Fort for dances, for medical help for themselves and their animals, and to get mail.

"And, of course, the Mounties were the police," he added. "People could come here for help if a horse got stolen, or if they had a disagreement with their neighbour."

Just then a train went by on the tracks to the south. It was very loud.

"That reminds me," laughed Duncan. "After the railway arrived in 1883, Calgary started to grow very quickly, and the Fort had to keep up. The Mounties tore down the original Fort and built the new barracks. By 1888 they had to build another one. Do you see the large white building with red trim next to the interpretive centre?"

The family turned to look back at the building. "This building is a reproduction of the 1888 barracks. It gives you an idea of how the Fort was changing." He showed them another picture with men playing cricket on a

A cricket match played on the grounds of Fort Calgary. The large white building in the right centre of the picture is the NWMP barracks. August 9, 1912.
Credit: Glenbow Archives NA-919-19

lawn in front of the barracks building. "This was taken in 1912. You can see that Calgary has grown enough to have power lines. On the left side is the house of Captain Richard Deane, who was the commanding officer at the time. We still have that house, but now it is across the Elbow River. You can visit it, and even get a meal at the restaurant."

He told them that in 1911, another railway reached Calgary. The city was becoming a major transportation hub, and people were buying up land in the hopes that it would increase in value as the city kept growing. The federal government sold Fort Calgary to the Grand Trunk Pacific Railway. In 1914 the men's barracks was torn down to make way for a rail yard. For the next 61 years, the birthplace of the city was hidden underneath warehouses and railway tracks.

"The only sign that it had once been Fort Calgary was a sandstone boulder with a plaque on it, donated by the veterans of the Mounted Police" said Duncan. "Let's walk down and see it."

They walked to the south west corner of the site, where a sandstone boulder stood next to four large red pillars with photos on them.

"How did the rail yard turn back into Fort Calgary?" asked Sarah.

"In the 1970s a man named John Ayer worked very hard to get the site

41

Fort Calgary covered in warehouses. The sandstone boulder is in the lower right hand corner of the picture.
Credit: Glenbow Archives PA-1999-15

restored to the people of Calgary in time for the city's centennial in 1975," said Duncan. "He was a City alderman, and he wrote dozens of letters to the federal and provincial governments, asking that they help buy Fort Calgary so it could be returned to Calgarians. In 1978 his work paid off when the interpretive centre opened."

He pointed to the four pillars. "That is his picture. We call him one of the four Sentinels, who help safeguard our history, and remind us of where we came from as a community. Beside him is Chief Crowfoot, representing the Blackfoot Confederacy. Next is Colonel Macleod, a friend of Crowfoot and the man who named the city. Finally, there is Captain Deane, the last commanding officer at Fort Calgary."

Sarah, Harry, Mom and Dad thanked Duncan and said goodbye. They went back into the interpretive centre to learn more about the Indigenous people, the North West Mounted Police, and other people who had built Calgary. After a busy day, they had lots to think about as they drove home.

Activities

1. Plan your own visit to Fort Calgary and the Deane House, across the Elbow River. Walk down to the confluence and imagine what it would have been like before there was a city here. Signs on the boulders explain some of the history of the Bow River. Outside the interpretive centre you will find a statue of a bison and another one of Colonel Macleod, as well as signs telling more about the history of Fort Calgary. Inside there are more exhibits and a video.

2. Walk across the George C. King Bridge from Fort Calgary to St. Patrick's Island. Corporal George King is sometimes called the first Calgarian because he was the first Mountie out of the boat when they crossed the river to start building the Fort. Read the sign at "King's Hideaway" on the island to learn more about him. You can also learn the Blackfoot names for local plants and animals.

3. Visit the Blackfoot Gallery at the Glenbow Museum to learn more about the history of the Blackfoot people.

Further Reading

The Blackfoot Gallery Committee. *The Story of the Blackfoot People: Niitsitapiisinni*. Richmond Hill: Firefly Books, 2013.

Canadian Museum of History. "Some Names in Southern Alberta" in *An Aboriginal Presence: Naming the Land.* Web article : http://www. historymuseum.ca/cmc/exhibitions/aborig/fp/fpz2d03e.shtml. Accessed September 21, 2015.

Deane, Richard Burton. *Mounted Police Life in Canada*. London; Toronto: Cassell and Co. 1916. Downloadable at the Internet Archive: https:// archive.org/details/mountedpolicelif00deanuoft.

Denny, Cecil. *Denny's Trek: A Mountie's Memoir of the March West*. Victoria: Heritage House, 2004.

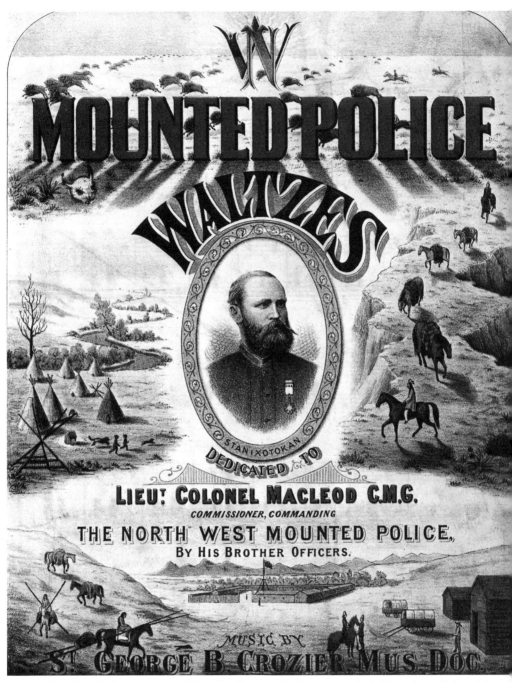

Mounted Police Waltzes composed by St. George B. Crozier and dedicated to Colonel Jame Macleod. Dated 1880. The composer's son, Inspector L.N.F. Crozier served in the NWMP unde Macleod.

Sound the Trumpet: The Story of Fred Bagley

Bob Pearson

Sarah's class visited the Glenbow Museum to see the exhibit called *Mavericks: An Incorrigible History of Alberta*. This exhibit tells the story of the adventurous, hard-working, and spirited men and women who built our province. The students were excited because their teacher said that a special surprise guest was coming, just to meet them. As the class walked off the elevator onto the third floor, they moved to the Mounties gallery. There they saw a man, dressed in an old-looking North West Mounted Police uniform. He had on black riding boots, light brown pants, a bright red jacket, and a funny-looking pillbox hat. In his white-gloved hand, he held a shiny brass bugle. As soon as the class walked in and sat on the floor in front of him, he began to speak.

"Welcome to the Northwest Territories. Come with me, back to a time before Alberta was a province, when Canada was very young, and so was I. When your teacher asked me to come and tell you about my life, I was a bit nervous. I mean, all this happened such a long time ago. My memory isn't that good anymore, but, luckily, I kept a diary so most of my adventures are written down.

"I guess I should introduce myself. My name is Frederick Augustus Bagley, but you can call me Fred. I was born in the British West Indies way back in 1858. My parents were British, and our family moved to England when I was just a baby. I went to school over there, and when I was ten,

45

Fred Bagley in his NWMP uniform, about 1880.
Credit: Glenbow Archives NA-3173-9

we moved once again, this time to Canada, where I lived for the rest of my life. We lived in the province of Ontario. By the time I was fifteen, I was a military trumpeter at the Royal School of Gunnery in Kingston.

"Now, before I continue, I should probably tell you what a trumpeter is. He is probably the most important man in any military group. He keeps everything on time. By blowing different little tunes, which are known as 'calls,' on a bugle or trumpet, he tells the rest of the men when to get up and when to go to bed. Actually, there are different calls for every part of the day. There's one for breakfast, lunch, and supper. Mail Call lets the troop know when there are letters from home. Stable Call tells the men that it is time to groom and care for their horses. Anyway, I think you get the idea. I know most of you have been to school, so think of the trumpeter as being like a school bell, keeping everyone on time all day long. Allow me to demonstrate." With that, Fred raised the bugle he had been holding to his lips and blew. The sound was loud and startled some of the students a bit. "Well, I'm a bit out of practice, but now I think you can see why the bugle was so good for getting the guys up and moving in the morning. Being a trumpeter in Kingston wasn't a bad life, but doing the same thing day after day was a bit boring. I wanted some excitement!

"At that time, Canada had only been a country for a very few years. Much

Much of it had yet to be explored, let alone settled. The Northwest Territories, which at that time included most of western Canada, had no law and order. Whisky traders, horse thieves, and cattle rustlers could come into this huge area of land and do just as they pleased. In fact, William Butler and others who explored the area told the government that they'd better do something about that, and quick. It wasn't long before reports of some horrible crimes reached Ottawa, the nation's capital. In 1873 Canada's first Prime Minister, Sir John A. Macdonald, decided to send out a police force to deal with the law breakers. Very soon, men were signing up to join the North West Mounted Police.

"Now, I liked to read, and the kind of thing I liked best were stories of adventure. My favourite writer was James Fenimore Cooper. He wrote a series of books called the *Leather Stocking Tales*. The hero of these books was a resourceful woodsman named Natty Bumppo. To read of his adventures and heroic deeds made me want to go forth and make my way on the frontier. When I heard that men were wanted for service in the North West Mounted Police, I decided to join up.

"To become a member of the force, a man had to know how to write in

The NWMP Band in Battleford, Saskatchewan in October 1884. Fred Bagley is in front holding a bugle and a sword.
Credit: Glenbow Archives NA-2328-1

either English or French. He had to be able to ride a horse and be between eighteen and forty years of age. Now I was only fifteen, but my mind was made up. I went to the fort in Toronto and signed on.

"My father was a good friend of Colonel George French, the commissioner of the force. When he heard what I was planning, Father ran to see the colonel to stop me from going. Father and I had a really big argument. Finally it was agreed that the colonel would take me on as a trumpeter for six months. I believe that my parents thought I would come running home with my tail between my legs in only a few days. But off I went. On May 1, 1874, one Frederick Augustus Bagley became the youngest member of the newly formed North West Mounted Police. After a month's training in Toronto, we left, all of us on the train. At the last minute, my mother handed me a blank diary, the same little book in which I wrote down my story.

"I thought that life in the West would be filled with excitement. I believed I'd spend my days riding wild mustangs and chasing whisky traders and horse thieves. Sure, I did have some adventures. I'll tell you about some of them. But it was mostly just the same thing, day after day. In fact, it was often just like the life I wanted to get away from in Kingston.

"Anyway, here's one story you might find exciting. We arrived and set up camp at a place called Dufferin, Manitoba. In the scramble to set up, I barely had time to say hello to my friends, Dick and Sam Steele, Jim Harding, and the others. One night while we were there, a terrible thunderstorm blew in. After one huge bolt of lightning struck inside the corral, the horses stampeded. They ran over six men. Luckily none of them was hurt too badly. The terrified animals scrambled and rolled over one another as they tried to get away. I remember the rolling thunder, the flashes of lightning, and the shouts of the troopers as they tried to stop the horses. I was trying to sleep in my tent, but it was suddenly trampled. It was my job to get the troops together by blowing the call for assembly. At first, I couldn't even find my riding boots. I climbed out from under my flattened tent in my bare feet and managed to play the call. When I finally found my boots and put them on, I quickly had to take them off because they were filled with water. Soaked and bruised, we spent a night in camp. In the morning, I got on one of the few horses that had not run away. After riding all day, we rounded up about eighty of our horses. When we rode into camp at about midnight, I was fast asleep in the saddle. I had to be lifted down and put to bed.

Fred Bagley (third from left) and the NWMP in London in 1897 on the occasion of Queen Victoria's Diamond Jubilee.
Credit: Glenbow Archives NA-2343-3

"Speaking of horses, do you remember me mentioning that I thought I'd be riding mustangs in the Mounted Police? Well, that wish did come true. I was strolling through our camp one afternoon when I noticed him, the mustang of my dreams. He was buckskin in colour and had a black streak down his backbone. The man who was holding his bridle was supposed to be guarding the camp, but he wasn't really paying very much attention. If the sergeant saw that, the fellow would surely be in trouble. This gave me an idea. I said to the man that if he would rather go and visit with his friends, I would take care of his horse. No sooner had he gone off than I took the mustang over to my troop and had him registered as mine. The man who had him before me couldn't do anything. He couldn't say that he had left his post and allowed me to walk off with his horse. The mustang's name was

Buck, and although I only had him for a short time, he was a member of the Mounted Police for as long as I was. Later, I heard that the man I had tricked said to some of the other guys, 'That boy Bagley is a natural-born horse thief, and he'll come to a bad end someday.'

"From Manitoba, we had to cross the prairies. This trip, which we took in the summer of 1874, would later be called the Great March West. You may ask why it was called a march when we were supposed to be riding horses. Well, the horses that we had were Thoroughbreds. They were used to warm stables and regular meals of oats and hay. They weren't used to eating the prairie grass and being outside all the time like my horse Buck. They really couldn't handle harsh conditions at all. So, we were often walking. Colonel French ordered the men to ride one hour then walk the next, in order to give our horses a rest. Even though Buck was a tough, strong animal, I was often on foot, too.

"One time, my feet were so sore that I took off my boots. One of the officers, I think it was Colonel Walker, saw me with my sore and bleeding feet. He picked me up and carried me into camp riding on his back. But at the end of the day, our feet were not too sore to dance to a tune played on a flute and a drum made out of an old cheese box. These were the only instruments we had, except for my trumpet and bugle. We were often homesick, and songs such as 'Home Sweet Home' brought us some comfort. Music would be the thing that brought me happiness for the rest of my life.

"We never had enough to eat. Our dinner was often just a meal of bread and tea. Sometimes, we ate something called hardtack. That was a kind of cracker that was made from flour, water, and salt. The reason we were given this was that it would last for a long time without going bad. It was very hard to chew and didn't taste all that great. There were also times when we were very low on water. I remember a day when my lips were so sore and blistered by heat and thirst that when Colonel French ordered me to sound a trumpet call, I could not play a single note. But it didn't stay hot and dry. By the end of the summer, it was so cold that we were all ordered to give up one of the two blankets we were given so that it could be used to cover up our horses.

By my sixteenth birthday, September 22, 1874, we woke up to find ourselves covered with snow. It was quite a sight to see the white of the snow and yet, the prairies were almost black with countless buffalo. By that time, we could see the Rocky Mountains and knew that our long journey was nearly over. Yes, the excitement I had read and dreamed about was only a small part of my life. Hunger, thirst, cold, and days filled with hard work were much more common.

"I have many more memories of my years in the Mounted Police. There was the time in September of 1877 that I and many other Mounted Policemen went to the signing of Treaty 7. Although I didn't really know it at the time, this was to be an important day in the history of Canada. Representatives of the British Crown and the Government of Canada met with the First Nations Peoples living in the area now called southern Alberta. There were five First Nations groups at the signing of the treaty. There was the Siksika (Blackfoot), the Kainai (Blood), the Piikani (Peigan), the Tsuut'ina (Sarcee), and the Nakoda (Stoney). For the First Nations Peoples, this was an agreement to share the vast plains with the newcomers from Europe. For the Government of Canada, however, the treaty meant the complete takeover of the First Nations' traditional lands. At the time, though, I was simply taken with the colour and excitement of the day.

"Being a lover of music, the thing that I remember best about that event was the North West Mounted Police brass band, which was led by Sergeant Major Tommie Lake. The band marched ahead of the colourful group of Siksika from their camp to the tent where the treaty was to be signed. This was an

Fred Bagley with his young daughter, about 1900.
Credit: Glenbow Archives NA-2564-4

51

important day for me. Not only was I at the very spot where history was being made, but I saw a small Mounted Police band. Soon, I would be in charge of bands like that, and they were very good, if I do say so myself.

"Even before I saw the band playing at the signing of Treaty 7, I had been part of several small musical groups of Mounted Police. There was the one we put together at Fort Saskatchewan. We had a drum, my trusty trumpet, two violins, two pot lids, part of a plough, and a few other things we put together. Now, I'm sure you're laughing to yourself to think of what that group sounded like and, you're right. It was a bit rough, but it was all we had, and to us, it sounded fine, well, sort of.

"For a while, I was stationed in Regina where I started a band that I was very proud of. It had brass instruments, violins, flutes, and a piano. The newspaper called it 'the best that was heard in Regina.' In time, I was transferred to Fort Calgary. As part of "E" Division, I was glad to find a large troop of men, many of whom were music lovers. I took charge right away and soon had a seventeen-man band organized. We put our money together and bought enough instruments for the group. We soon got to be so good that we could play while marching or on horseback. Sometimes, playing on horseback didn't go so well. More than once a frightened horse galloped away from the rest of us, throwing its rider in one direction and his trumpet in another. The people of the growing town of Calgary came to love our band. They lined the streets to watch and listen to our daily mounted parades, which went through the downtown streets during the summer months. Once, we played at a grand ball at the brand new Banff Springs Hotel in honour of the Governor General, Lord Stanley of Preston. And, if you were a part of the band, you were often allowed to skip some routine duties, like cleaning the stables, in order to practice.

"Don't think that all I did was play music. By the time I retired from the North West Mounted Police, I was a sergeant major. Not too bad for a guy who started out as a lowly trumpeter at the age of fifteen. And those six months that my father said I could be on the force actually lasted for twenty-five years. More important, I got married. I and my wife Lucy-May even started a family. In 1897 I was one of the men chosen to go to London for the Diamond Jubilee of Her Majesty, Queen Victoria. That was one of my greatest honours. The year I retired, my faithful old mustang Buck died. He was thirty-two years old, a ripe old age for a horse.

"Just because I was no longer with the force didn't mean that I stopped playing music. In fact, I played more than ever. Music was very important to people at that time. There was no television or even radio. There were a few record players, but they were very expensive and there weren't very many records made yet. If you wanted music, you played it yourself or came to listen to somebody else play. It was considered a sign that you were a person of good taste if you had a piano. My friend, Roy, who was also a musician, said that if somebody moved to Calgary and 'didn't have a piano, you didn't think much of them.' Many people had musical evenings. They would have some friends over, sit around the piano, and sing. Every town and city had a bandstand. These were big stages, usually with a roof over them to keep off the rain and hot sun. Bands like mine would give concerts in the summer. People would come, often bringing a picnic lunch. No doubt about it. Music was very important, and I did my best to provide as much of it as possible.

"Calgary has changed a lot. You have no idea how it looked over a hundred years ago! Probably the biggest bandstand in the city stood where the Palliser Hotel is today. Now, I wouldn't want you to think that I was the only one who played music in Calgary at that time. My good friend Crispin Smith organized and led the Fire Department Band. Like me, he gave concerts and marched with his band at many important occasions, such as the Calgary Stampede Parade.

"I helped start an army band. It was called the 15th Light Horse Regimental Band. Once, a band came to Calgary from Ireland. We welcomed them and made them feel right at home. They played a few concerts, and when they left, they asked us to come to Ireland and play at the Irish International Exhibition. This was an offer too good to pass up. We raised enough money, and soon, all fifty-three of us were on our way. We played concerts right across Canada and on the ship. In Ireland we played twice a

Fred Bagley leading the Calgary Citizens' Band down Second Street SE in 1910. Parade was in recognition of King George V becoming the King of Britain and other countries of the Commonwealth, including Canada.
Credit: Glenbow Archives NA-4277-12

day at the exhibition. I think you could say that the audience liked our music, for after our final performance, my friend Colonel James Walker and I were carried off the stage on the shoulders of the crowd. We completed our tour with concerts in England before returning home to Calgary.

"Calgary grew very fast in its early years. Just as it is today, the city was bursting with local pride. There was no better way to celebrate that pride than to have a citizens' band. The band was formed in 1902. When I returned home from Ireland, I became bandmaster. The forty-eight band members looked splendid in their navy-blue uniforms, trimmed with black silk cord and capes, all topped off with shiny peaked caps. All this cost a lot of money, but the people of Calgary were very generous and helped out as much as they could. Sometimes, we would play loudly outside the home of some important person who might help us to raise more money. We were a part of almost every important occasion. Each year on Victoria Day, we took the train to Banff and played an outdoor concert. We even got to play at a formal ball in honour of the Prince of Wales, who visited Calgary in 1919.

54

"Some say that I was a natural-born musician. If you'll excuse the joke, I don't want to blow my own horn, but I did a lot for music in the West. I even got to be pretty good on the clarinet. During my days in the Mounted Police, I had been stationed in Banff for a while. My wife and I fell in love with the little mountain town and we moved there after I retired. Lucy-May rented cabins to visitors in order to make a little money. I worked greeting guests at the beautiful Banff Springs Hotel. I even wrote a book about my adventures as a Mountie.

"I'm glad you let me tell my story. I think you'll agree that although times have changed, cities have gotten bigger, there are more things to do and more people to do them, that people themselves are pretty much the same. Just like you, I longed for adventure and ached to do great things. As you get older, you, too, will have many interesting stories to tell. I hope that when it is time to tell them that there will be good friends like you to share them with. Before you leave, take some time and look around the Mounties gallery. You will see some of the things that I have saved over the years. I'm glad they are here in the museum, helping to bring my story to life."

With that, the man in the historic uniform said, "Now, I would be glad to answer a few questions."

Sarah's friend Kristin was the first to raise her hand. "You're not really Fred Bagley, are you?" she asked.

"Well, I'm an actor. I bring Fred Bagley to life and tell his story so that people today can feel what it was like to live many years ago."

Scott asked, "How do you know what Fred's life was like?"

"Fred left us a diary and pieces of a book that he was writing," said the actor. "Then there are records left by the North-West Mounted Police, letters and all sorts of other clues I use to help me bring Fred to life. By now, I think I know him pretty well."

"We have time for one more question," said the teacher.

Caitlyn put up her hand and asked, "Fred, were there any women in the Mounted Police?"

"Not at that time," he said. "When the force was called the North West

Mounted Police, women weren't allowed in. Today, the Royal Canadian Mounted Police have many opportunities for women."

"Well," said Sarah's teacher, "I think we should thank Fred Bagley for allowing us to share in his exciting adventures." The class stood and clapped. They then moved on to see the rest of the *Mavericks* exhibit. They discovered the stories of explorers, rodeo stars, wrestlers, politicians, pilots, business people, and many other men and women who made Alberta such a great province in which to live.

Activities

1. Visit the Glenbow Museum in Calgary. There you will find the *Mavericks: An Incorrigible History of Alberta* exhibit. See what things are on display that bring Fred Bagley's exciting story to life.

2. While you are in the area, stroll down Ninth Avenue and visit Fort Calgary. There, you will be able to try on a uniform very much like the one Fred Bagley wore. You can also discover how Fred and his fellow Mounties helped build the city of Calgary.

3. Read *The Leather Stocking Tales* by James Fenimore Cooper. It was a favourite of Fred Bagley's and I think you'll see why it made him long for a life of adventure in the West.

4. If your school has a band, ask the teacher if you can try blowing into the mouthpiece of a trumpet. Ask the teacher to show you how it's done. Try to imagine doing that during freezing-cold weather as Fred did.

5. Keep a diary of your own. Some day it might help people to know how you lived, what you liked to do, and what your hopes and dreams were. Remember that you are a living part of history so make your mark.

Further Reading

Glenbow Museum, "Mounties," *Mavericks: An Incorrigible History of Alberta*, Student Resources, Accessed May 1, 2015, http://www.glenbow.org/mavericks/student/english/thm_moun/links.html.

For more information about Fred Bagley including his diary, unpublished book (*The 74 Mounties: The Great March across the Plains*), photographs, and letters, visit the Glenbow Museum online at, http://www.glenbow.org/collections/search/findingAids/ archhtm/bagley.cfm.

For information on Treaty 7, check out this site. It has a good, short history of the treaty and how it has impacted Canadian society. Accessed May 14, 2015. http://wayback.archive-it. org/2217/20101208160337/http://www.albertasource.ca/treaty7// index.html#.

Engine 29 was the last steam engine in CPR regular passenger and excursion service.
Built in 1887, it was placed on display on Calgary's 9th Avenue in 1996.
Credit: Walt DeBoni

The Railway Comes to Town

Rob Lennard

The big day had finally arrived, and Sarah and Harry could hardly contain their excitement. They waited anxiously to board the vintage Royal Canadian Train, located in the majestic Canadian Pacific Pavilion, adjacent to the historic Fairmont Palliser Hotel in downtown Calgary.

It was August 11, and their favourite relative, their great-grandfather "Engineer Eddy," who drove trains for Canadian Pacific Railway for close to fifty years, was celebrating his ninetieth birthday.

"Wow, Great-Grandpa Eddy," Sarah declared, "it's fantastic that CP Rail gave you three passes on the historic train to Banff and back to celebrate your big birthday. Harry and I are thrilled that you are taking us!"

Engine 147 after pulling a passenger train from Winnipeg to Calgary in 1884.
Credit: Glenbow Archives NA-967-12

"Kids," their great-grandfather smiled, "the big reason I chose you two to come along was because I rode the train for the very first time when I was about your age.

"I'll never forget it," he continued with a smile. "It was on Canada Day that I travelled to Regina to see the King of England with my monarchy-loving Aunt Victoria, who was named after the mother of Princess Louise Caroline Alberta, the beautiful princess our great province is named after.

"The minute the train left the station," Eddy reminisced, "I was overcome with joy. I knew right there and then that I wanted to be a locomotive engineer and drive trains when I got older!"

A moment later a loud, high-pitched train whistle blew, startling all the passengers. The many tourists from all around the world quickly turned their heads toward the tall and friendly train conductor dressed in his vintage blue and burgundy uniform, standing outside the entrance to railcar number four.

Driving the last spike on the Canadian Pacific Railway, Craigellachie, British Columbia, November 7, 1885. Men numbered in photo: 1. W.C. Van Horne 2. Sandford Fleming 3. D.A. Smith 4. J.H. McTavish 5. J.M. Egan 6. James Ross.
Credit: Glenbow Archives NA-218-2

"Ladies and gentlemen, boys and girls," the conductor bellowed in his Scottish accent, "my name is Billy Van Horn, and I would like to welcome you to the one and only incredible Royal Canadian Train, which is comprised of locomotives that were used over sixty years ago, and beautiful rail cars that date back close to one hundred years.

"Also, if you are wondering if I am related to the famous William Cornelius Van Horne, the former president of the Canadian Pacific Railway who oversaw the building of the transcontinental railroad and attended the Last Spike ceremony at Craigellachie, British Columbia, at 9:22 am on November 7, 1885, I hate to disappoint you, but I am not."

Billy continued, "Before you board the majestic train, I thought I would mention that we have some very special guests on board. We have Jim and Heather Higgs, celebrating their fiftieth wedding anniversary. We have three couples from Europe, Asia, and Mexico on their honeymoons, and we have "Engineer Eddy," a long-time locomotive engineer with Canadian Pacific Railway who is celebrating his ninetieth birthday today! Eddy's birthday happens to coincide with the exact date that CP Rail first rolled into Calgary back in 1883."

Billy looked down at his gold pocket watch, saw that it was 8:53 am, and yelled out, "All aboard, folks! We depart Calgary in exactly seven minutes and fourteen seconds!"

A few minutes later, just as Sarah, Harry, and their great-grandfather were about to board the train, a familiar voice was heard.

"Hey, Eddy, where do you think you are going?" a man in his sixties, wearing an engineer's cap shouted out. Eddy turned around and to his pleasant surprise saw that the man who was talking to him was none other than Max Ellis, the engineer of the Royal Canadian Train, the same engineer he had helped teach back in the early 1970s.

In his right hand, the engineer held three CP Rail engineer caps, which he proceeded to hand out to Eddy and his great-grandchildren. "Okay, put your hats on folks and follow me," he declared. "You three get to ride up in the locomotive with me this morning!"

The first permanent CPR railway station in Calgary.
Credit: Glenbow Archives NA-1497-11

As the four walked toward the front of the train and the steps leading up into the locomotive, Eddy and the kids were beaming with excitement.

Once inside, the excitement turned into sheer euphoria as Sarah and Harry got to blow the loud train horn at precisely 9:00 am, while their great-grandfather took to the controls of a locomotive for the first time in over two decades. Moments later, the Royal Canadian was heading west on a ribbon of steel toward Banff and the beautiful Rocky Mountains.

"Eddy," Max yelled over the chugging locomotive, "I'll never forget my first day of locomotive training with you when you bent the rules and let me drive your train three days before I passed my final test. I figure it's high time that I returned the favour and let you drive my train for the first fifteen minutes or so today."

Eddy beamed. "Max, what an amazing birthday present! Quite frankly," he continued, "I thought the next train I would be driving would be the one stopping off at the pearly gates after I kicked the bucket!" he chuckled.

Max then turned and faced Sarah and her brother and asked, "Okay kids, while your great-grandpa is at the controls, are there any questions you two have for me? The railroad is in my blood, starting with my great-grandfather, Fred, who shovelled coal on the first locomotive that arrived in Calgary way back in 1883, twenty-two years before Alberta became a province."

This was the first railway station in Calgary – an old boxcar that was taken off its wheels.
Credit: Glenbow Archives NA-659-18

"Well," Harry piped up, "any idea what Calgary was like when the railway first arrived?"

"Let's see," replied Max, "according to my great-grandfather's log book, in August 1883, the village of Calgary consisted of a grand total of eight hotels, including The Far West Hotel, three billiard halls, six laundries, ten stores, and a photographer – all in tents!"

"All in tents? You've got to kidding!" replied Harry.

"So just how big was the celebration when the train rolled into town, Engineer Max?" Sarah asked.

"Well, young lady, after the four-hundred-strong construction crew of graders, spike men, and track layers busted their butts for the contractor, Langdon and Sheppard, between Medicine Hat and Calgary, including laying a world record of more than fourteen and a half kilometres of track in one day, they were ready for a big celebration. Especially since their contract had finished in Calgary, and they were all paid off in full."

"Wow," Harry interjected. "I can only imagine how they spent their money after all that back-breaking work!"

"No need to imagine Harry. According to the log book, there were running races with bets reaching into the thousands of dollars, horse races where at least $5,000 changed hands, and a wheel of fortune that raked in hundreds of dollars!"

"Goes to show you," the engineer chuckled, "that gambling in Calgary started way before Lotto Max tickets were sold.

"Okay, Eddy," Max shouted, "we are now approaching the bend in the track that takes us down by Bowness Park, so it's best that I take over the controls before somebody at the park reports a retired ninety-year-old engineer driving the Royal Canadian and I get fired!"

The Royal Canadian Pacific consists of 10 Canadian Pacific Railway 1920s era business cars coupled to two 1950s locomotives all of which have been restored to their original splendor. This train was put into service in 2000.
Credit: Walt DeBoni

A few seconds after Max took over the controls from Eddy, he pulled hard on the seldom-used emergency brakes, producing a loud and unforgettable screeching sound that could be heard throughout the popular northwest Calgary park, as well as lots of bright fiery sparks that burst from the metal locomotive wheels. At the same time, Sarah and Harry took turns frantically blowing the loud train horn.

"What the heck is going on here, Max?" Eddy yelled out at the top of his lungs as the train came to a screeching halt. "Was it a moose or baby carriage on the tracks, or a broken rail, or worse?"

Before anxious Eddy could finish his sentence, however, more than one hundred people young and old suddenly appeared from the park, carrying helium-inflated birthday balloons and yelling out in unison, "SURPRISE! HAPPY BIRTHDAY, EDDY!"

Sarah and her brother yelled out with glee, "We got ya, Great-Grandpa Eddy!"

The interior of the lounge car of the Royal Canadian Pacific. Dignitaries such as J.F. Kennedy, Winston Churchill and Queen Elizabeth II have traveled in this car.
Credit: Walt DeBoni

Max spoke up with a smile, "Eddy, my friend, we started planning this big surprise party for you last winter, and everyone was in on it, including the two hundred passengers who were told to expect screeching brakes soon after the train departed and not to worry."

Eddy responded, "You've got to be kidding. I am speechless!"

"Now," Max smiled, "it's time for the three of you to get the heck off my train and go enjoy the party these folks have planned for you in the park. Also, don't feel like you've been shortchanged on the trip—one of your grandkids will be driving you up to Banff later on today to catch the train ride back home with me tonight."

With that, the three adventurers disembarked and headed down to the park to enjoy Eddy's humongous locomotive-shaped chocolate birthday cake. Both Harry and Sarah were already thinking about perhaps following in their great-grandfather's footsteps someday and riding the "ribbon of steel."

Activities

1. Ride the steam train at Heritage Park.
2. Attend Canada's largest model train show, held in Calgary each year! For more information see www.supertrain.ca.

Further Reading

Berton, Pierre. *The Last Spike*. Random House of Canada Limited. Toronto: Random House, 1971.

Dempsey, Hugh A. *Calgary: Spirit of the West*. Saskatoon: Fifth House, 1994.

The former office of the Eau Claire and Bow River Lumber Company is now a cafe near the site of the original mill.
Credit: Walt DeBoni

We Needed Lumber: Peter Prince Delivered

Irene DeBoni

It was Saturday morning and Harry and Sarah had just had their swimming lesson at the Gray Family Eau Claire YMCA. Their parents arrived to pick them up.

"How was swimming today?"

"Great," said Harry. Without pausing, he said, "I'm starved." (This was pretty normal for Harry.)

"Actually, I'm pretty hungry myself," said Dad. "What do you say we all go over to the Buffalo 1886 Café for brunch? One of my co-workers told me it is a great place to go."

"I'm always up for going out," said Mom.

"But where is it?" asked Sarah.

"That white building that looks like a house in the centre of the square," said Dad.

"Really? That's a restaurant?" asked Sarah. "It sure looks kind of out of place among all these newer buildings." With that, they stepped inside.

As the hostess seated them, they all looked around. "Wow," said Harry. "Look at the buffalo heads. And look at the old clocks. And what's with all the money on the walls?"

The hostess, Dannie, gave them menus and smiled. "This building actually dates from 1886 and was the office building of the Eau Claire and Bow River Lumber Company. A picture from 1890 shows it with a flat roof,

The Eau Claire and Bow River Lumber Company office in the 1890s. Notice on the left side, in front of the office, a man riding what appears to be a tricycle with one large wheel and two smaller wheels.
Credit: Glenbow Archives NA-422-2

but otherwise it was the same then as it is today. Starting in 1893, it also became the office of the Calgary Water Power Company. So this building was the place where bills for lumber or power were paid.

"It has been a restaurant for many years. It's fun to see where customers are from, so people have sent us money from their home countries. And the clocks, well, one of the owners thought the antique clocks fit the mood of the building."

Just then, two men walked in. One was a chef from Campbell River coming to Calgary to celebrate his birthday with his family. "I worked here thirty years ago," he said. "Back then, all the walls were coated with money. We had the menu up on that blackboard. Omelettes. That's all we served, so even though the name was the same as it is now, we called it the Omelette Café. Still the original tin ceiling; that was hard to paint! Oh, and look, the original safe, actually the first safe in Calgary, is still over there in that corner."

Dannie smiled, "We still have the original key to the door of that safe; not sure where it is though. Go and have a look."

Sarah and Harry quickly went to the open doorway and peeked in. They had gone on trips with their parents and stayed in hotels with safes in the rooms, but this was not at all the same. This one was like a big pantry. "Ketchup!" Harry exclaimed.

"Yes," said Dannie, "that is where we store all of our condiments. But when this was the Eau Claire Lumber Company office, all of the important documents and cash would have been kept in the safe. Fires happened quite often in the early days, and the wooden buildings would burn quickly, so it was important to have a fire-proof safe to keep important papers."

She then told them an interesting fact: Calgary's first vault robbery took place in that very building. The robber blew up a stick of dynamite against the outside wall. He was caught on horseback on the Tenth Street bridge.

Back at their table, the family placed their order and looked at the back of the menu. There they found a summary of Peter A. Prince and his accomplishments. He...

- was manager of Eau Claire and Bow River Lumber Company;
- built Calgary's first skyscraper: the Robin Hood Mills site (now Gulf Canada Square);
- built the first water wheel on the Bow River, which supplied Calgary with electricity through the Calgary Water Power Company (until 1926 when it was taken over by Calgary Power Company);
- invented and patented the Sheerboom, an important piece of logging equipment used to secure logs;
- built a public transport bridge across the Bow River near the present-day Louise Bridge;
- was president of Calgary Iron Works and partner in the large Prince–Kerr Ranch near Brooks (still owned by Prince's relatives);
- bought and learned to drive a 1903 Red Rambler, the first gas-powered car in Calgary – when he was eighty years old; and
- built one of the first architecturally designed brick homes in Calgary, located at Fourth Avenue and Second Street (the house is now in Heritage Park).

A smile broke out on Sarah's face. "That's where I know the name from. That's my favourite house in Heritage Park. I love the room with all the doll furniture and the little tea sets. Who do you suppose played in that room?"

"Perhaps the room is just made up to look like a child played there,"

The photograph was taken in about 1896. The Prince house was located at 238-Fourth Avenue SW, just across the street from today's Jamieson Place office tower that is named after Alice Jamieson, another famous Calgary pioneer.
Credit: Glenbow Archives NA-1360-3

commented Mom. "We know that Mr. Prince and his first wife Margaret had two children, John and Rosanna, but they were already adults when the family came to Calgary. Unfortunately, for Mr. Prince, his wife died. He was married three more times, but he didn't have any more children. His last wife, Emily, did have a daughter, Nora, but she also was older. In fact, the only things in that house that actually belonged to the Prince family are in the dining room. So Heritage Park obtained the rest of the furniture from other homes of the same period. Fun to think about someone playing with all of those things, though, isn't it!"

"But how come the house is in Heritage Park?" Harry asked.

"This used to be a huge residential area," said Dad, "but the land became very valuable. Two of Prince's grandchildren, Ruth Wise and Leslie Longpre, sold the property. In 1966 Alberta and Southern Natural Gas and Alberta Natural Gas donated the house to Heritage Park, and in 1967 the house was reconstructed there. Office towers soon replaced the houses in Eau Claire, and recently condos and hotels have been built."

Peter Prince built this house in 1894. It was moved to Heritage Park in 1967, where it resides today.
Credit: Walt DeBoni

"Yeah," said Harry. "And now we know why it is called 'Prince's Island Park.'"

Dannie brought their drinks and said, "We have some old pictures downstairs. Why don't you go down and have a look while you are waiting for your eggs."

With that, the family walked into the adjacent room, past the back door and went down the stairs into the basement.

"Oh, my gosh, look at these pictures! Some of them are from the 1800s. Look, there is Mr. Prince in his car. In fact, there are several pictures of his cars. He must have really liked cars. Can you believe he learned to drive when he was eighty? That is like a dinosaur's age!" Harry said.

"Well, not quite," Dad smiled.

"Some of these people are from Wisconsin," noted Mom. "I know there is an Eau Claire in Wisconsin. Is there a connection here somehow?"

"Good thing I have my iPad," said Harry as he Googled it. After a few searches, he found that Eau Claire is the singular form of the French name, Eaux Claire meaning "clear waters" for the Eau Claire River. Supposedly French explorers travelling down the muddy Chippewa River in Wisconsin came across the "Eau Claire" river and exclaimed "*Voici l'eau claire*" ("Here is clear water!").

A logjam on the Bow River. These logs are on their way to the Eau Claire and Bow River Lumber Company sawmill in Calgary.
Credit: Glenbow Archives NA-1360-8

Sarah chimed in, "The Bow River is usually clear, too, except when it floods like it did in 2013."

"My gosh," said Harry, looking down at his iPad, "there sure is a lot of information here. Can you explain some of this, Dad?"

Dad looked at the iPad and silently read the information. "Well," he said, "it looks like a lawyer from Ontario whose name was MacFee realized that Calgary would need lumber to build houses and stores. This was because people would start to arrive on the new railway that reached Calgary in 1883."

Dad paused and looked at Sarah and Harry and asked, "Why would people need lumber? Couldn't they just cut down some trees?"

Harry and Sarah thought about that. "I've got it," said Sarah. "When we did a tour of Nose Hill, the guide told us that this area didn't have trees, just grass."

"Exactly," said Dad. "But Mr. MacFee knew there was lumber in the Kananaskis. Trouble was, he didn't know how to get it.

"What do you do if you don't know something?" Dad smiled at them.

Harry thought Dad was teasing him. "Okay, okay. We ask you or Mom or our teachers," he said.

"Well," Dad continued, "Mr. MacFee knew some lumbermen in Eau Claire, Wisconsin, so he went to them for advice on building a lumber company. They became enthusiastic about the possibilities in this newly opened up part of Canada. In fact, they decided to form a new company called the Eau Claire and Bow River Lumber Company." Dad grinned at them. "Guess they called it that since they were in Eau Claire, Wisconsin. Anyway, the plan was to get permission to cut down logs in the Kananaskis and float them down the Bow River to Calgary. They would saw them into lumber at a mill they would build by the Bow River. Peter Prince was the manager of this new company, and Isaac Kerr was the president."

"And there's a picture of Mr. Kerr," said Sarah. "And remember, when we cross the bridge to go into Prince's Island, it says that we are on Kerr Plaza."

"That's right, Sarah," said Dad, and he continued with the story of the Eau

Claire Lumber Company. "Soon, a crew of Norwegian workers disassembled a mill in Wisconsin and shipped it to Winnipeg, in Canada. There, the mill was put onto a CPR train and went west. The lumbermen and the mill arrived in Calgary in June 1886. The workers lived in tents while putting the mill back together again. These skilled workers helped to produce lumber, built their own homes, and raised their families near the mill."

"But why here?" Sarah asked.

Harry, looking over his dad's shoulder, read from the iPad, "The Eau Claire and Bow River Lumber Company dug a channel, designed by Peter Prince (hey, that's the lagoon now) to get logs from the Kananaskis closer to the sawmill. In doing so, he created an island. At its peak, the lumber mill made three railway carloads of lumber every day."

Young men beside the Eau Claire and Bow River Lumber Company sawmill.
Credit: Glenbow Archives NA-4277-4

76

"You mean the same lagoon where we go skating every winter? And watch the ducks and geese the rest of the year? And where we spend hours riding our bikes around in the summer?" Sarah asked.

"Yes," said Mom. "The mill operated until 1944, and in 1947 the descendants of Peter Prince donated the land to develop a park."

"That explains the pictures of the lumber mill and even the tent," said Sarah.

"And that explains why there is a little white church that we drive by on Third Avenue when we are driving home," said Mom. "The Norwegian families would have attended that church. In fact, I think I read that it was originally called the Norwegian Lutheran Church but now is just Trinity Lutheran."

Peter Prince in a Red Rambler car with son John Prince at the wheel. This car is said to be the first one in Calgary to use gasoline, brought in by John Prince in 1903 and owned by him until 1905.
Credit: Glenbow Archives NA-1952-1

"It's too bad that most of the mill workers' homes were torn down," said Sarah.

"Well," said Mom, "most of them were torn down in order to make room for the big office towers you see around us. But there is another home in Heritage Park that belonged to a Norwegian mill worker, named Bernt Thorpe. His youngest daughter donated the house to Heritage Park in 1969, as well as the funds necessary to restore it."

"Wow. So Heritage Park became the home for more than one house that had belonged to workers who worked in the lumber industry," Sarah said.

"Hm," said Dad. "I'm sure our food has arrived by now. Let's go eat. And perhaps when we get home, we can find out more information about Peter Prince and some of his projects."

Activities

1. Visit the Prince House and the Thorpe house in Heritage Park. What do the homes tell us about the way the people lived? Do you think there were servants? When you are in the Prince House, you will notice that the house was built from plans in the *Scientific American, Architects and Builders Edition*. Ask your parents how they chose your house, condo, or apartment.

2. Do you like solving puzzles? Figuring out family history is like doing puzzles. One clue leads to another.
   a. Visit St. Mary's Cemetery in Calgary. See if you can find the Prince family plot. Whose names are on the marker? When did they live?
   b. Now go to Union Cemetery. Can you find more of the Prince family? Why do you suppose they are in two separate cemeteries?
   c. See what you can learn about the Prince family from searching for Peter Anthony Prince on the Internet.
   d. Go to the library and ask an adult (perhaps a parent or the librarian) to help you use ancestry.ca. Now, do a search on Peter Anthony Prince. Where was he born? When did he go to Wisconsin? What were the names of his wives?

3. Go to the original address of the Prince House, 128, Fourth Avenue SW. What is there now? Try to imagine homes in this area instead of office towers and condos. Where would children have gone to school?
4. Have you ever moved or lived in a different city? What do you think it was like for the Prince family and their children to move from Ontario to Wisconsin to Calgary?

Further Reading

"Prince, Peter Anthony." Ancestry.ca. Accessed May 2015. www.ancestry.ca. (Especially genealogical records and census records.)

Sons of Norway. "The Norwegians in Calgary." Accessed May 2015. http://sofncalgary.ca/about/.

The cupola of the James Short School, originally called Central Public School. The school was built in 1904 and closed in 1968.
Credit: Walt DeBoni

For Whom the Bell Tolls: Calgary's First Schools

Valerie Walker

Sarah and Harry were on a walking tour of Calgary. They were doing some research for school, and their parents thought it would be fun to check out the oldest surviving school building.

They drove to Haultain Park at the corner of Thirteenth Avenue and Second Street SW. They parked the car and walked over to the old sandstone building. "Wow, I bet that old place could tell some stories," said eleven-year-old Sarah.

The original two-room South Ward School renamed Haultain School when a 10-room school was added beside it.
Credit: Glenbow Archives NA-613-1

Harry and their parents had caught up to her. "It is a charming building, isn't it?" said their dad. "The unique architecture is known as Richardsonian Romanesque."

"That's a fancy name," said nine-year-old Harry.

"It sounds quite romantic," said Sarah. "There's an inscription over the door. Haultain School 1892-1922." She was busy taking pictures from all angles. "I really like the roof. Can we go inside?"

"Well, don't be too disappointed. It is now used as an office for the City of Calgary. It was used as a two-room school until 1907."

When Sarah had finished taking photos, they rang the bell and were let in by a friendly woman. "I'm sorry, there are no tours today. How can I help you?"

Sarah explained they were doing research on the school.

"Well," said the woman, "it was built in 1892, and a larger school was built beside it when it became apparent that more room was needed. Unfortunately, the new school burned down in 1964. In 1972 the smaller school was still intact, and it was leased to The City of Calgary by the school board and designated as a Registered Historic Resource. Some time before

The 10-room Haultain School, about 1913. It was destroyed in a fire in 1964.
Credit: Glenbow Archives NA-5610-80

the city renovated it and turned it into offices, it was used as a school for the blind."

"I'm so glad it was saved," said Sarah. "It must have been fun being taught in a two-room school."

"I'm sure it was. It was the first school to have electricity and running water. When the second school was built, both schools' names were changed to commemorate the memory of Sir Frederick Haultain, the president of the Executive Council of the Northwest Territories Legislative Assembly – kind of like Alberta's premier. The larger school was eventually closed in 1962, two years before the fire." She gave them some pamphlets to take home then said, "It wasn't the first school to be built in Calgary, though."

"Oh, where is the first school?" asked Harry.

"Can we see it?" asked Sarah.

"Well, that might be difficult. It has quite a history. I don't have all the information, but you may be able to find it in the city's archives."

Sarah and Harry were very disappointed but thanked the woman for her time and went back out into the warm sunshine. "I hope we can find some information on the very first school," said Sarah. "That would be amazing."

A grade 5 class in the Haultain School, 1910.
Credit: Glenbow Archives NA-4370-2

"Excuse me," said a voice. They turned to see a well-dressed gentleman. He doffed his hat and said, "I couldn't help overhearing that you are interested in learning about Calgary's first school."

"Oh, do you have some information?" asked Sarah.

"As a matter of fact, I do. Shall we move over to a bench in the shade?"

"Thank you, sir," said Sarah's father, "that would be wonderful."

They walked down the path until they found a suitable bench. Sarah and Harry sat on the grass, leaving the bench for the adults.

The gentleman settled himself comfortably, cleared his throat, and began. "There has been a great deal of confusion about buildings, folklore, and rumours about the school. However, in July 1998, a group of historians painstakingly put together conclusive documentary evidence and facts, along with photographic proof, that the school was in fact established in Inglewood, at 538, Ninth Avenue SE."

"Is it still there?" interrupted Harry.

"Sadly, no. It has had a long and mysterious history. In 1883 the *Calgary Herald* published an article about the need for a school in Calgary. The railroad had arrived, and with it many more settlers. The *Herald* suggested raising money through a collection, or to pass the hat, then demand the Northwest Territories Council match the local funding with an equal sum so that sufficient funds could be raised to supply a good school in Calgary.

"In 1884 a meeting was held to establish a legal school division. Calgary's population was approaching five hundred, and on February 18, 1884, the first public school opened for twelve students. It was a small shack, supposedly built in 1883. It was described by a local historian, Frederick C. Hunter, as hardly being fit for human habitation and would be more suitable for use as a hen house than a school house, but at least Calgary had a school."

Sarah and Harry laughed. "Imagine having to go to school in a hen house!"

"Indeed, it must have been very cramped. Local carpenters made rough tables and benches that served as desks, and the children shared the few books and maps that were available. They wrote on slates."

"Slates!" exclaimed Harry. "Why?"

"In the old days, all children wrote with chalk on pieces of slate. It was much cheaper than paper and pencils, and was easily available."

"What about teachers?" asked Sarah.

"At first, there was one teacher, John William Costello. He was brother to William Nolan Costello, who was one of the school trustees. The story goes he had enough children to populate the school. One of his children became a mayor of Calgary, Dr. Michael Copps Costello. He was mayor during the war years of 1915-1918. John Costello had to resign as teacher when funds ran out. After a brief interval, classes resumed in May 1884, when a new teacher was found, James Spencer Douglas.

"Calgary was a real cow-town in those days, and on one occasion, the whole school was given a half-day off to attend a First Nations powwow. This was a special event where the local First Nations got together to join in song and dance. They visited with old friends and made new ones. It was a time to exchange stories and to keep traditions alive. These events were often private, but sometimes they were made public, so it would have been a real treat for the schoolchildren to witness this special gathering.

"Cowboys also rode their bucking broncs everywhere, much to the delight of the school children, who together with their teacher, rushed outside to see the daring riders who stuck to their saddles and brought their fiery steeds under control."

"I wish I had gone to school then," said Harry. "It sounds like a lot of fun."

"Oh, it was," said the gentleman. "Calgary was the real Wild West in those days.

"By May 1884 the school had a class of thirty-two children. Calgary was growing fast and enrollment was increasing, so the unincorporated school board had to put on an addition, but even with the added room, quarters were cramped. By the end of school term in June, there were fifty students, and when classes ended, so did the building's five months' occupancy as a schoolhouse."

"Only five months?" said Sarah. "All that work and it was only used for five months. How sad. What happened next?"

"Well, the school board had to find new facilities."

"But what happened to the old school?" asked Harry.

Hockey team, Haultain School, 1939-40.
Credit: Glenbow Archives PB-303-3

Drama group, Haultain School, about 1930-49.
Credit: Glenbow Archives PB-303-6

"Well, one of the trustees, Howard Douglas, bought it and divided the large structure into smaller rooms and used it as a family home. Later, it was sold to an absentee landlord, a young military officer and former Mountie. It changed hands several times and was rented out to many different people. Unfortunately, it was also the site of a sensational murder."

"How dreadful," said Sarah.

"Yes, that rather put a damper on it being used as a residence, and so it was used as an auto-body shop. The owners, unfortunately, left it full of storage, and then boarded it up and left it to fall into rack and ruin."

"But that is so sad," said Sarah. "Did it fall down?"

"Not quite," said the gentleman. "It was bought by William Costello, another son of the first schoolteacher, and it was repaired and rented out to various occupants. The last was a respected pioneer who spent the winters in Arizona. It gradually fell into disrepair, though, and was left to rot.

"By 1950 it was slated for demolition to make room for a new project in our fast-growing city. The mayor at the time, Donald H. Mackay, had no idea of the building's historic value. Demolition had started when it came to the attention of James Braehead Cross, who saved about two-thirds of it and had the structure moved to the Calgary Brewing and Malting Plant, together with the damaged portion, with the intention of reconstructing it as a museum of Old Canadiana."

The gentleman sat back and looked at the children. "I hope that answers most of your questions."

"Not quite," said Sarah. "Did it actually become a museum, and can we see it?"

"Not much is known about it after it was moved. James Cross was on the board of the Calgary brewery, but one of his pet projects was the fish aquarium built in 1960. In May 1963, The Horseman's Hall of Fame was built on the brewery grounds and filled with historical exhibits, and it was a popular place for schoolchildren to visit.

"The aquarium was closed in 1972, and the hall of fame was closed in 1975, and all its artifacts were moved to the Glenbow Museum. The brewery

87

was closed in 1994, and now there is talk of the brewery being demolished. As yet, I have been unable to discover the fate of the old schoolhouse. However, I do have this, which may interest you." The old gentleman stood up and handed the children a photo together with some notes. They were all so busy reading that when Sarah turned to thank the gentleman for all the information, he had disappeared.

"He's gone! Harry, Mom, Dad, did you see where he went?"

They all shook their heads. "What a shame," said Dad. "He didn't even tell us his name."

"He was so interesting. I didn't realize Calgary's schoolhouse history was so exciting," said Sarah.

"Neither did I," said Harry. "Now we need to do more research."

"He was certainly very knowledgeable. He spoke as if he had been there, didn't he?" said Sarah.

"Yes, I could almost see it happening as he spoke," Harry agreed.

Harry's father looked at the notes the gentleman had left them. "Well, there is a little more information on other schools here that might be helpful." He shuffled the notes. "Listen to this. Also in 1885, St. Mary's Girls School was opened in a two-story log cabin. The Riel Rebellion had forced the sisters of the Faithful Companions of Jesus to move farther west and they settled in Calgary."

"Probably the very first all-girls school," said Sarah. "Neat!"

"In 1886," continued Dad, "a wooden school with a brick front was built on today's site of the James Short Parkade off Centre Street in downtown Calgary. It was known as Central School and with the growing population soon became full, and students had to take classes in nearby churches, and even the roller skating rink."

"They had a roller skating rink back then?" asked Harry. "Does it say anything more about that?"

"No, I'm afraid not, Harry. In 1884 the South Ward School, which is this school here, now renamed Haultain, opened its classes for the September enrollment. It didn't meet Calgary's needs for very long. Between 1906 and 1915, attendance in Calgary schools soared from 2,050 to 11,100 students."

Harry was busy calculating. "Wow, that's an increase of more than nine thousand children!"

"Well, it doesn't stop there," said his father. "Eighteen cottage schools were built around the city to keep up with the boom."

"What are cottage schools?" asked Sarah.

"They were two-story buildings built in residential neighbourhoods.

Seventeen two-story wooden schools were built between 1910-1912 to meet the needs of a booming population. The one pictured here, the Hillhurst Cottage school is one of only three remaining.
Credit: Walt DeBoni

They were built to fit in with the houses around them. There's one in West Hillhurst we can go and look at if you like."

"That would be great," said Sarah. "What else do the notes say?"

"Calgary built nineteen splendid sandstone structures between 1902 and 1912. The King Edward School at 1729 Thirtieth Avenue SW was built from sandstone taken from the quarry at Seventeenth Avenue. It cost $172,000 to build then, more than $3 million in today's money."

King Edward School, a sandstone school built in 1912.
Credit: Walt DeBoni

"I guess that's where the sandstone came from for the Colonel Walker School as well," said Sarah.

"I'm sure it did," said her father. "In 1906 the first Calgary Normal School was opened. This teacher-training school became part of the University of Alberta Faculty of Education in 1945. In 1922 the province built a fancy new campus for the Institute of Technology and Art on the North Hill, today's Southern Alberta Institute of Technology and the Alberta College of Art and Design."

He sat back and looked at Sarah and Harry. "Well, that's a lot of information to take in, isn't it?"

"It's a good thing we have notes," said Harry.

"I wonder if we'll ever see that kind gentleman again," said Sarah. "He was so helpful; I would like to thank him."

"He must be a local historian. Perhaps he just enjoys helping children learn about Calgary's local history," said her father.

"Yes, that must be it. But I really would like to know what happened to Calgary's first school. It is quite a mystery," said Sarah.

"Can we go and see the cottage school in Hillhurst now?" asked Harry.

Dad nodded and smiled at their mother. "This has been very interesting, don't you think?"

"It certainly has, I don't think we are going to have to nag our children to work on this project," Mom said.

The family made their way to the car, but Sarah turned to scan the park one more time in the hope that the knowledgeable gentleman might still be around.

Activities

1. Take a walking tour of Calgary and see how many sandstone buildings you can find. How many of them are or were schools?
2. Visit the schoolhouse in Heritage Park. How many desks are there? Does it have a chalk board?
3. Visit the Glenbow Museum. How many exhibits can you find that relate to early Calgary schools?
4. Have your parents help you find some pieces of slate. Meet with your friends and hold a mock class using the slate and chalk instead of paper and pencil.
5. Arrange with your friends and their parents to visit as many "cottage" schools as you can find. You may have to do a little research to find out where they are. The Hillhurst Cottage School that Sarah and Harry visited is at 455, Twelfth Avenue NW.

Further Reading

Calgary's first school: Type "the true and correct history of Calgary's first school" into your browser to find out more about Calgary's first school.

Haultain School: See http://www.historicplaces.ca/en/rep-reg/place-lieu. aspx?id=5104. (Or type "Haultain School" into your browser.)

Powwows: For more information on powwows, see http://www.powwows. com/what-is-a-pow/wow/.

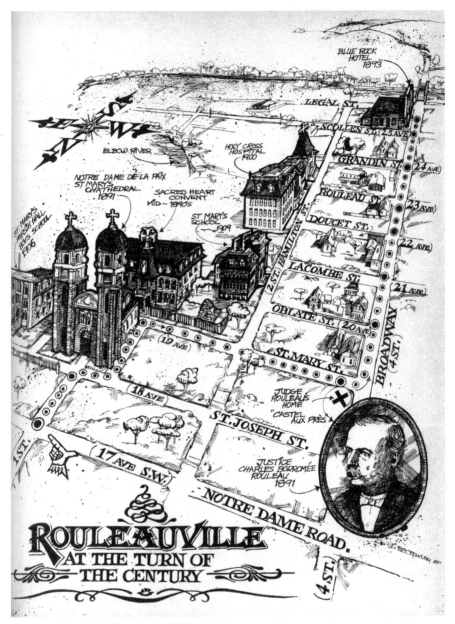

A map of Rouleauville, about 1900, showing some of the more important buildings at the time. Note the names of the streets.
Credit: Glenbow Archives LIB-9-1

Ici On Parle Français

Elizabeth Marshall

"You mean that here in Calgary there are lots more people than you, *Grand-mère*, who speak French all the time?" Ten-year-old Suzanne, a friend of Sarah's, looked up at her grandmother in surprise. It was a warm, sunny July day, and they were walking out of the Holy Cross Hospital where they had just left Suzanne's mother at her medical appointment.

"*Mais, bien sûr!*" answered *Grand-mère*. "This part of the Mission area of Calgary was once known as Rouleauville, and most of the people living and working here spoke French." They sat down on a bench in front of the hospital entrance, in a pretty little garden arranged around statues of two women. "Why, French-speaking people set up this very hospital."

"Really?" asked Suzanne. "In all the times that we have come here, Mom never told me that."

"*Eh bien, c'est vrai.* Well over a hundred years ago, Roman Catholic Bishop Grandin, who lived in St. Albert, just north of Edmonton, but who worked all over Alberta and Saskatchewan, saw that the people living around Fort Calgary needed doctors, nurses, and a hospital. He went to Montreal to ask the Grey Nuns to help him set up medical care, both in Edmonton and here in Calgary. In 1891 four very brave women came to get this hospital started. The head of the new hospital was Sister Agnes Margaret Carroll. She was Irish, but the other three nuns were French-Canadians. Sister Beauchemin was a trained pharmacist, and Sisters Valiquette and Beimer were experienced nurses. A small two-storey log building was used as the hospital and their home. It was ready and waiting for them when they arrived."

"And they made it into a hospital all by themselves?" asked Suzanne, suddenly wondering how four people could do all that without help.

"*Pas exactement*," *Grand-mère* explained. "The day after they arrived, their new neighbours never stopped knocking on their door, bringing them towels, sheets, blankets, and everything else they thought the Sisters might

Construction of the Holy Cross Hospital began in 1892 with several additions over the years. This is a photo of the oldest remaining part of the hospital, added in 1928. The hospital closed in 1996.
Credit: Walt DeBoni

need to get started. The Sisters planted a large garden – you know, they had to prepare all the meals for their patients as well as for themselves. Sister Carroll asked everyone living in the area to donate what money they could. She also made and sold apple pies at fairs to earn money for the hospital. By the end of their first year here, they had already added on to their building, and two Sisters had spent four weeks taking care of patients with smallpox, who had to be kept away from everyone else, in a tent on Nose Creek. The next year, there were so many diphtheria patients that the Sisters gave up their own beds to the people needing their care. It wasn't long before they also set up a school of nursing. These statues show a nun and a student. I don't know what the people living here would have done when they were ill if the Grey Nuns hadn't come to Calgary!"

"Wow, that's amazing! And did some of their patients speak French?"

"*Mais, oui! La plupart*! A great number of the people living in Fort Calgary at that time spoke French," *Grand-mère* assured her. "And the Grey Nuns weren't the only ones to come a long way to help people living here. I

St. Mary's School original name in stone. The original brick and stone school was torn down in 2002 and replaced with a new school named Our Lady of Lourdes. Some of the original stones were used in the new school.
Credit: Walt DeBoni

think we've got time to walk up the street and I'll tell you about another interesting group of women in our history."

"Oh, *oui, s'il vous plaît, Grand-mère.*" Suzanne enjoyed using the bit of French she knew when she was with her grandmother. "Which way will we go?"

"Just a little way up Second Street." After a couple of blocks, they stopped in front of Our Lady of Lourdes School. "Look up above the red brick entrance. Do you see a brown sandstone block above the door?"

"Yes!" exclaimed Suzanne. "It says 'St. Mary's School 1909.'"

"*Oui, c'est ça*," agreed *Grand-mère*. "But the first classes were held long before that, in other buildings just around the corner. Let's go on and find a place to sit down – it's kind of a long story."

Suzanne was eager to hear another of *Grand-mère*'s tales, and they strolled along to Nineteenth Avenue where Suzanne was amazed to see a large stone building that looked like it would be more at home in northern France than on the Canadian prairies.

"Who lives here?" she asked. "It looks quite old, and they must be a very rich family."

"It's not a house for one family," *Grand-mère* corrected her, "but in a way, it does belong to *une famille*. They are the group I want to tell you about."

They kept walking to the end of the large yard around the building and found a bench in a little park. "This story begins in France, in 1820, in Amiens, a small city just a short distance from Paris," *Grand-mère* explained. Suzanne leaned closer: she felt that this was going to be an interesting tale.

"A very rich noble lady set up an order of nuns, *Les Fidèles Compagnes de Jésus*, the Faithful Companions of Jesus," *Grand-mère* continued. "They were to set up schools, in France and in faraway lands, and also to teach adults. In just a few years after its Revolution, France became a dangerous place for noble people and this lady fled to England where she set up the same order of nuns. Bishop Grandin, in St. Albert, heard about these nuns and thought that they would be very useful on the prairies because they could teach in both French and English. He wrote to the Mother Superior, begging her to send some of her teachers to Canada. *Mère Petit* knew that the trip would be long, hard, costly, and even dangerous, and that Bishop Grandin did not have the money to help pay for the nuns' travel. It would be very hard for her nuns, but she promised that they would do it, for God! In 1883 eight teachers, four who spoke French and four who spoke English, arrived by ship in Montreal. Bishop Grandin was there to meet them. They spent over two years in Manitoba and Saskatchewan, getting to know what their work on the

The FCJ Convent as it looks today. The original school run by the FCJ nuns was in a log building located on this site in 1885.
Credit: Walt DeBoni

prairies would be like, and they finally arrived in Fort Calgary in 1885. In just one month, they had their school, St. Mary's, ready to open."

"And that's the St. Mary's school we just passed?" asked an excited Suzanne.

"Well, that was the name of their school," explained *Grand-mère*, "but it started out in a small log building where this large building is today. At that time, nuns often taught only girls, but since there was no other school in Fort Calgary, they took boys, too, but in separate classrooms. Most of their students were Métis who had French-speaking fathers and First Nations mothers, but English-speaking families sent their children there, too. In 1893 they built part of this beautiful building, and it has been rebuilt and made bigger many times. *Les Fidèles Compagnes de Jésus* still work here, teaching classes to adults."

Suzanne sighed. "But what I don't understand, *Grand-mère*, is how so many French-speaking people came to be living in Fort Calgary. How did they get here?"

"Let's walk over to the little bridge over the Elbow River, Suzanne. Rivers are a big part of Alberta's history." Suzanne was even more puzzled, but she followed her grandmother to stand in the middle of the bridge, looking down on the shallow and calm waters.

The railway bridge over the Elbow River. You can see the original St. Mary's Cathedral in the upper left of the picture.
Credit: Glenbow Archives ND-8-306

"If we go way, way back in Alberta's history, we learn that explorers from France and from Quebec were the first to meet First Nations peoples on the Canadian prairies as they paddled their canoes along our rivers. In the early 1740s, Pierre Gaultier de Varennes, Sieur de La Verendry, from Trois Rivières, Quebec, was in charge of all the fur-trading posts on the prairies. At that time, these explorers had no idea how much land lay to the west of their forts, but they wanted to find that out. La Verendry sent his sons and a nephew farther west to see what was there. We don't know exactly how far they got, but some people think that they may have seen the Rocky Mountains. We do know that another fur trader from Quebec, Joseph Boucher, Chevalier de Niverville, sent some of his men to explore the Saskatchewan River, but we don't know if it was the North or South Saskatchewan or how far west they got. Another explorer, Jacques Le Gardeur de Saint-Pierre, said that on one of his trips he had seen *des montagnes de roche*, mountains of rock. They then became known as the Rocky Mountains. After the British took over France's land in North America in 1763, many French-speaking fur traders decided not to return to France or to Quebec. Some worked for themselves, buying and selling furs wherever they could across the prairies. Many signed on to work for the Hudson's Bay Company as fur traders and guides – *les voyageurs*. Because of their skills and because they knew the area, voyageurs were part of every exploring trip in the West. Some decided that they would rather stay around Fort Calgary than be on the move all the time. They often married First Nations women and set up homes in this area. By the 1880s, many were working as 'bull train' drivers. They drove long caravans of wagons, pulled by oxen, from Fort Benton, Montana, all the way to Edmonton to deliver the goods needed by new settlers in the area. Their children were most of the pupils in the St. Mary's School."

Suzanne was silent, trying to imagine a big group of French-speaking people living around Fort Calgary. As she looked up at her grandmother, she noticed a very old house, its windows and doors boarded up, sitting at the end of the bridge. "Do you have a story about that old house, *Grand-mère?*" she asked.

A drawing of Charles Rouleau's house. The house was torn down in 1940 to make way for an apartment building.
Credit: Glenbow Archives NA-5222-3

Grand-mère peered up to where Suzanne was pointing. "Oh, you mean the Rouleau house!" she exclaimed. "*Mais oui, chérie*! That house belonged to Édouard Rouleau, one of two brothers who were famous French speakers living here in this part of Fort Calgary. Let's go closer and have a look." As the two neared the building, *Grand-mère* explained: "Charles Rouleau was a lawyer who moved to Fort Calgary to become the first trained judge to live here. Shortly after, his brother, Édouard, a doctor, came to join him to care for the North West Mounted Police. When the Holy Cross Hospital opened, he was the chief of staff. People in Fort Calgary were very pleased to have a judge and a doctor living in their town, and these brothers soon became leaders in the community. A village called Rouleauville was formed in this very area – come just a few steps farther to see the park where their story is told."

As they came to the park, Suzanne suddenly looked up at a huge tower. "Wow, what a beautiful building," she breathed.

The sign at Rouleauville Square where today we honour the history of this community. The images of Charles and Édouard Rouleau are in the centre of the sign.
Credit: Walt DeBoni

"Yes, that's St. Mary's Cathedral. Fathers Doucet, Fourmand, and Scollen first built a mission called *Notre Dame de la Paix*, Our Lady of Peace, near Bragg Creek. A few years later, they built another one here to help about five hundred French-speaking families living in Fort Calgary in the late 1880s. The village of Rouleauville was formed in 1889 and went from the Stampede grounds over to Fourth Street SW, and from Seventeenth Avenue SW down to the Elbow River. It became part of Calgary in 1907." *Grand-mère* suddenly looked at her watch. "Oh! We'd better be getting back to the hospital. Your mother will be waiting for us. We can look at the old French street names as we go."

As the two walked along, they stopped to look carefully at the special street signs in the Mission area and took turns calling out the French names that the streets used to have, starting with Seventeenth Avenue: Notre Dame, St. Joseph, St. Mary, Oblate, Lacombe, Doucet, Rouleau, Grandin, Scollen, and Legal. Suzanne listened carefully as *Grand-mère* said the names in French, and she repeated them to

A modern street sign that includes both the current street number and the historic name.
Credit: Walt DeBoni

101

get them just right. At last, they turned into the same little park in front of the Holy Cross Hospital where they had been sitting. Suzanne's mother was waiting for them.

"Oh, don't tell me!" Suzanne's mother exclaimed. "You two have been off on an adventure again! You can tell me all about it in the car."

Activities

1. On a street map of Calgary, trace the area that was once Rouleauville, as *Grand-mère* describes it, and try to locate the Holy Cross Hospital, *Les Fidèles Compagnes de Jésus* convent, St. Mary's Cathedral, and Rouleau Square. Some day you may want to try to follow the path that Suzanne and *Grand-mère* walked.

2. On a map of Canada, trace the route of the Grey Nuns from Montreal to Calgary. They would have been on a Canadian Pacific Railway train.

3. On a map of the world, trace the route of *Les Fidèles Compagnes de Jésus* from Liverpool, England, to Montreal, Winnipeg, Portage la Prairie, Batoche (a little northeast of Saskatoon), and Prince Albert in Saskatchewan and, finally, to Calgary.

4. Ask your parents to take you to visit the place where Fathers Doucet and Scollen built the first *Notre Dame de la Paix* mission. It's on the west side of Highway 22, just north of Bragg Creek. There is a little sign pointing to it, but you will have to watch carefully.

5. If your school or public library has a book on the fur traders (voyageurs) or the Hudson's Bay Company, you may find that it is an exciting and interesting read.

Further Reading

Alberta Online Encyclopedia. "Oblates in the West: The Alberta Story." Accessed May 12, 2015. http://oblatesinthewest.library.ualberta.ca//eng/.

Dempsey, Hugh A., ed. *The Best from Alberta History*. Saskatoon: Western Producer Prairie Books, 1981.

Dempsey, Hugh A. "Mutiny at Ft. Calgary." *Alberta History* 53, no. 3 (Summer 2005): 9-12.

Dempsey, Hugh A. "The Day Alberta Went Dry." *Alberta History* 58, no. 2 (Spring 2010): 10-16.

Hoffman, Barbara. "Women of God: The Faithful Companions of Jesus." *Alberta History* 43, no. 4 (Autumn 1995): 2-12.

MacEwan, Grant. *Between the Red and the Rockies*. Toronto: University of Toronto Press, 1952. (See especially Chapter 1 about the early explorers.)

MacGregor, James G. *A History of Alberta*. Edmonton: Hurtig Publishers, 1972.

Sanders, Harry. *Historic Walks of Calgary*. Calgary: Red Deer Press, 2005. (See especially the walk through the Mission area.)

The Menorah is the symbol of light in the Jewish faith. The Menorah must be lit in every Jewish home during the Hanukkah holiday.
Credit: Walt DeBoni

Building the House of Jacob: Jacob Diamond and Congregation House of Jacob

Agnes Romer Segal

Sarah and her younger brother Harry burst noisily through the front door, kicking off their boots and shrugging off their backpacks and parkas. Within minutes they were in the warm kitchen, excitedly chattering at their mother as Sarah pushed a small package into her hands. "So can we go?" they asked in unison.

"Whoa!" Mom exclaimed as she placed the package on the table and wiped her hands on her apron. "I did not catch a word you were saying. Why don't you try again, one at a time, and then I'll open this surprise." The children looked at each other, and reluctantly Harry closed his open mouth and let Sarah explain.

"Today, my friend Esther's mom, Mrs. Gold, came to my class to teach us about Hanukkah. It is the Jewish holiday that's celebrated in the winter. It celebrates a victory ages ago when the Jews overcame their Syrian-Greek oppressors and were able to rededicate their temple and continue to practice their religion. Anyway, they celebrate for eight days by lighting candles in a menorah and eating food cooked with oil..."

Harry could not wait for her to finish. He burst in, "And we are invited to their party this Sunday. Can we go?"

Sarah jabbed her elbow into his arm. "I was getting to that, but first I want to explain the package – if you'll let me." Harry looked down at his feet, partly in apology and partly in displeasure. "So," Sarah continued, "Mrs. Gold made latkes with us. Those are the potato patties they eat, and that's what I brought home for you to taste. She also invited the class to come to the Hanukkah party at their synagogue this Sunday evening if we want to see how they celebrate. I told Harry all about it. Can we go?"

"And can we eat those latkes now?" asked Harry, who had just about lost all his patience.

As they ate the latkes their mom had reheated, Sarah showed her mom the recipe and explained why they were considered Hanukkah food. They phoned Esther's mother and made plans to meet at the synagogue the following Sunday.

As they drove south on Fourteenth Street toward the synagogue building, they passed the turn off to Heritage Park, and Sarah suddenly shouted, "Look there's a menorah beside those old trains lit up for Hanukkah!" To their surprise, they passed another set of bright lights, this time atop the Calgary Jewish Centre, just a block before they reached the synagogue parking lot.

"Hey, I remember I used to have swimming lessons there," remarked Harry.

Esther was waiting for them at the entrance of the synagogue. "I've saved us some seats in the social hall," she said. "Come, I want to show you something before we sit down." On the side of the entrance doors, they stopped beside a model building mounted on a base. It was bigger than a large dollhouse, taller than Harry, actually. It was red brick with an interesting front, decorated at the top with a six-pointed star and the words "House of Jacob," and at the very top, the number 5671.

"Who is Jacob, and why is his house so important that you have a model of it here?" asked Harry as he inspected the large model.

Esther chuckled, "You are not the first to ask that. I did too, and my mother told me that in fact, the city building inspector was also confused when he saw the building plans. He asked 'What in thunder do you want to plaster the man's name all over the plans for? I don't care whose house it is as long as it complies with the building by-law.' Actually, Jacob is the Jacob

The House of Jacob, 1967.
Credit: Jewish Historical Society of Southern Alberta, C.L. Arbour Photographer.

you know from the Bible. Many synagogues all over the world are named in honour of our forefather Jacob. This is a model of the first synagogue to be built in Calgary, the original building of this congregation. But Jacob is also Jacob Diamond, and in a way, this was also his house. He was largely responsible for getting it built."

Sarah, looking puzzled, asked her friend, "So Esther, has your family been in Calgary for several generations? Most of the other Jewish kids I know moved here from other places not so long ago."

Esther nodded, "Yes, many Jewish families came to Calgary from Europe and other parts of Canada and even the Soviet Union and Israel throughout the past hundred years, but Jacob and Rachel Diamond were the very first Jews to settle in Calgary. They arrived from Ontario in 1889. Two of Jacob's brothers followed him to this area a few years later. There was nothing here for Jewish people in those days, except the opportunity to live freely, and that was something they did not have in their old communities in Europe a century ago."

The interior of the House of Jacob, 1967.
Credit: Jewish Historical Society of Southern Alberta, Matthews Studio and Photo Lab.

Harry had been listening carefully as he walked around the model and looked at the sanctuary beyond. "You mean he and his wife were the only Jewish people here for many years? Why did they stay here? Didn't they want to celebrate holidays with other people just like them, just like you are doing here?"

"Good question, Harry," Esther answered. "I've asked my mom the same thing. She called Jacob a pioneer, just like the first settlers who came and broke the ground for farms and cities."

Esther's mom came up to the children to call them to the celebrations. She nodded at Esther's answer and continued, "Well, he really was a pioneer. There is even a photo of him on the wall of the building of the Southern Alberta Pioneers and their Descendants, among the portraits of all the other pioneers who settled here before December 31,1890. Jacob had left his home in what was then Russia to avoid being forced to serve in the czar's army. He managed to make his way to England and lived there for a while until he could afford passage to North America to find a better life. He always loved all things English. Apparently, he even looked like King George V. He gradually worked his way west, peddling furs and other things. In Ontario he met Mary Stoodley. She converted to Judaism and became Rachel Diamond when they married. They went on to have five children. Rachel's sister had moved to Calgary upon her marriage to a member of the Mounted Police. Jacob must have understood the enormous opportunity Calgary held. He started off trading hides in partnership with his neighbour, but over the years he owned a grocery and then a liquor store, until Prohibition ruled that all liquor sales be shut down. I've seen a photo of the crowds viewing the first Stampede parade in 1912, showing Jacob with his two daughters standing outside his store on what is now Olympic Plaza. Jacob retired early and devoted himself to family and community. Those first years must have been hard and lonely, but Jacob did not allow himself to be isolated. He had learned to speak English in England, and he became involved in the society around him. He became an active member of the Odd Fellows and the Masonic Lodges, which did a lot of public good. One early Calgary newspaper article called him 'a live wire.'"

Rachel and Jacob Diamond about 1890.
Credit: Jewish Historical Society of Southern Alberta

"Couldn't he have just become like everyone else, without the Jewish rituals, if they let him become a member?" asked Harry.

"I think he could have, if that is what he had wanted. But being Jewish and being free were important to him. He knew that a Jewish life meant being part of a Jewish community, and he did what he could to build one," Mrs. Gold answered. "He went out of his way to help those Jews who made their way to this area, some just for trade and others to try to settle on the land. He organized the first Jewish prayer groups either in his own home or in rented places. Often, he led the services himself. Just like settlers from other backgrounds, Jews continued to come from eastern Canada and even from the States to take advantage of the economic opportunities that the developing West offered. With increasing numbers, Jacob was able to build his community of Jews. In 1904 a local Jewish baby died, and he approached the city to buy some land for a Jewish cemetery. That cemetery grew and is now full. We had to develop a new one recently. By 1909 there were enough Jews here to form a community that met regularly, and we still have the written minutes of those meetings. Jacob served as their first president, and he went on to be elected president seven more times! They decided to buy land first to build a small space for prayer services and for classes to teach their children about their religion and then to erect a lovely synagogue. Together they decided to name their synagogue House of Jacob. Jacob Diamond was so pleased that on the spot he pledged the first donation toward the building. Then began the hard work of raising funds for the building."

"So when was this synagogue built, and where was it? What street was number 5671 on?" Sarah asked.

Esther chuckled again, "5671 wasn't the address. That is the date for the year 1911 according to our Hebrew calendar. The building was opened at 323 Fifth Avenue E in time for the Jewish High Holidays in autumn of that year. That was the area where most Jewish families lived at that time. You won't find the original building there anymore. It was torn down in 1968, when the entire city centre was redeveloped. Older people here still remember that building. It's where Bow Valley College stands today, and Jewish people live all over the city now. That is why we have this model. We had it built for our congregation's hundredth anniversary float for the 2009 Stampede Parade. Come, I'll show you something else." And she dragged Sarah by the arm, out the front door. She pointed to a stone at the base of the building. "This is the original cornerstone from the 1911 building. R.B. Bennett, who later became Canada's prime minister,

Rose and Hattie Diamond, the daughters of Rachel and Jacob, about 1908.
Credit: Jewish Historical Society of Southern Alberta

was at the ceremony when it was set into the ground. I have a newspaper clipping about it at my house."

Shivering, they ran back inside to join the festivities. After the Hebrew blessings and songs and the lighting of the candles, they were warmed by the steaming latkes and other goodies. As they munched on chocolate coins, Esther taught them a traditional game using a small spinning top she called a *dreidl*. As Harry watched the top spin around and around, he thought about how amazing it was that over 120 years ago Jacob Diamond had come to a Calgary without any Jews, and now there were so many Jewish children all around him, happily celebrating a Jewish holiday. All because Jacob had stuck with his dream of building a house for his community.

Activities

1. Visit the Montefiore Institute at Heritage Park. It served as synagogue in an early Jewish farming colony near Sibbald, Alberta. Often there are special cultural activities at the institute. During the Once Upon a Christmas featured at Heritage Park, there are usually Jewish cultural activities related to Hanukkah.

2. House of Jacob-Mikveh Israel hosts school groups if plans are made in advance. Ask your teacher if she would like to arrange a class visit. Alternatively, there is a more exact, smaller model of the House of Jacob in the Calgary Jewish Centre, 1607 Ninetieth Avenue SW.

3. The Jewish Historical Society of Southern Alberta makes classroom visits. The people from the society can tell you more about local Jewish history.

4. Make your own latkes. Following is a recipe that doesn't require modern appliances.

Latkes

6 potatoes, pared	1 small onion, grated
3 eggs	1 teaspoon salt
¼ teaspoon pepper	¼ cup flour
1 tablespoon oil	2 teaspoons baking powder
oil for frying	

Grate the potatoes and squeeze out extra liquid to drain well. Blend in remaining ingredients. Drop from a spoon into hot oil and brown on both sides, turning only once. Yield: about 2 dozen latkes.

Source: Jewish Women International of Canada, Mount Sinai Chapter #1091. *Second Helpings, Please!* Montreal, 1998.

Further Reading

The House that Jacob Built.: Congregation House of Jacob-Mikveh Israel Calgary, Alberta Centennial Commemorative Book. Calgary: Congregation House of Jacob-Mikveh Israel, 2009.

A Joyful Harvest: Celebrating the Jewish contribution to Southern Alberta Life, 1889-2005. Calgary: Jewish Historical Society of Southern Alberta, 2007.

An image of a captivated reader that would have thrilled Annie Davidson.
Credit: Photo illustration by Walt DeBoni

The Dream of Annie Davidson

Christine Hayes

Sarah and Harry were at the Shawnessy Library, participating in the annual Lego Challenge when they noticed a sign talking about the library's hundredth birthday.

"Weird," said Sarah. "I thought this library was new."

The librarian overheard her comment and said, "This library is new but it is just one of the newest of our community libraries. Right now we have seventeen different libraries in Calgary, but the first one was built in 1912."

"Wow! What did a library look like in 1912? They didn't have computers, I'll bet!"

"You're right, no computers. But come with me," the librarian said. She

Calgary Public Library about 1912.
Credit: Calgary Public Library CPL_103-21-01

115

led them to a computer. "You can see pictures of the original library right here." She opened up a site on the library's home page and showed Sarah and Harry a picture of a small sandstone building in the middle of an empty park. "This is the first Calgary Public Library," she said.

"That is so cool!" said Sarah. "Where is that library? They didn't knock it down, did they?"

"No, the library is still standing, and next Saturday there will be a celebration of the building's one-hundredth birthday."

"I want to go," said Sarah.

"Me too," Harry chimed in.

So, on the day of the birthday party, Sarah and Harry headed down to the Beltline area and made their way to Central Memorial Park. This was the first time they had been to this part of town, and they were surprised to find such a beautiful park right in the middle of high rises and condominiums. At the front of the park, just behind the war memorial, they saw a beautiful sandstone building. The kids recognized it from the pictures the librarian at Shawnessy had shown them. They were kind of surprised by its size – it

Circulation desk in the library where one checked out the books being borrowed, about 1912.
Credit: Calgary Public Library CPL_103-28-01

seemed small. But it did look old and kind of fancy for a library. They stood at the bottom of the wide stairs and looked at the beautiful carvings over the doorway. Harry noticed that there was an open book carved into the stone.

Stepping inside the library was almost like going through a time machine, even though there were computers on the desks. The walls and the paneling looked like it must have in 1912 when the library was new.

The kids had a feeling they were being watched and turned to look at the closet in the entryway. Staring out at them was an old lady wearing old-fashioned clothes.

"Whoa! Who is that?" they said at the same time, a little startled by the big face in the door.

"Librarians know all kinds of weird stuff, " said Sarah. "We'll ask the librarian."

The library was small inside and was split into different rooms, but it was cozy, and the kids felt like they'd like to grab a book and settle down in one of the armchairs by the fireplace to read. But there was a party to go to so they headed down the staircase by the front door to the basement, where they could hear the sounds of celebration.

Annie Davidson, the lady that started it all.
Credit: Calgary Public Library

In the basement they found balloons and streamers and people talking and having a good time. There was a giant cake in the middle of the room, and photographs lined the walls.

"There she is!" yelled Harry, pointing to a photo on the wall.

The librarian who was serving the cake gave them a big smile.

"Her name is Annie Davidson,

and she is the lady who is responsible for the creation of this library," he said. "Take a piece of cake and head to the room next door. We have a speaker who is going to talk about Annie and the beginning of the Calgary Public Library."

Sarah and Harry took their cake and went to the room across the hall. Lots of people were there, waiting for a man with a moustache to start talking. The crowd settled down and the man began to speak.

"Welcome," he said. "It is wonderful to see you all here. I am going to tell you the story of a determined woman, her friends in a book club, and the founding of this amazing library."

The man started up his computer, and up popped the picture of Annie Davidson.

"Annie Davidson was born Annie McKean in New Brunswick in about 1832. She married her husband, Richard, in September 1862. Richard was a merchant whose business was selling supplies to the ships leaving St. John. Over the years, Richard and Annie had ten children, but life was much harder then, and several of their children didn't survive. Richard was very successful for a while, but in 1881 business was so bad that he had to declare bankruptcy. This made life really difficult for the Davidson family, but Annie loved to read and she found that books always made her feel better about things.

"Hoping to start over again, Richard moved the family to Brandon, Manitoba. Things weren't great, but there were opportunities there for their children, and many of them were able to get good jobs. In 1897, though, Richard died. Some of Annie's children had moved to Calgary by this time, so she decided, in 1906, to join them.

"Who knows how many people live in Calgary today?" the man asked the audience.

Several hands shot up.

"Over a million people," said a boy in the audience.

"Right," said the presenter. "There are 1.2 million people in Calgary today. But when Annie came, there were only 43,000 people living here. Calgary was a kind of baby city that was just starting to grow. You can see in

Looking east along Stephen Avenue in 1906.
Credit: Calgary Public Library PC_743

the picture that the sidewalks were made of wood and the streets were paved with dirt.

"There weren't a lot of really fancy buildings and this neighbourhood, where the park is, was where people with lots of money lived. People like Senator Lougheed, who was a lawyer and built the Lougheed House along with other buildings in the downtown, like the one in this picture.

"Even these streets in this neighbourhood were just dirt roads and the park that this library is in was just a bit of land with no gardens and only spindly little trees.

"As I said before, Annie always felt better when she was reading so when she got to Calgary, one of the first things she did was to start a book club with other women who liked to read. They met at Annie's house, which was very near to here on Thirteenth Avenue West, to talk about the books they read. This group became known as the Calgary Women's Literary Club, and the members decided very early on that they were going to do everything they could to create a public library for Calgary.

"There were already some libraries in Calgary at the time, but they

The Sherman Grand, built by Sir James Lougheed in downtown Calgary in 1912.
Credit: Calgary Public Library PC_253f

were private, like Senator Lougheed's large library, or they charged for memberships, like the library in the Herald building. There were also book shops, but the ladies of the literary club knew that to make books available for everyone, the library had to be free and open to the public.

"The government at the time believed the same thing, and it passed a law saying that if 10 per cent of the electors (who are the people who are allowed to vote in an election) signed a petition, the government would look into building a library. Now, at this time only women who owned property were allowed to vote, so the literary ladies couldn't even sign their own petition. They had to go and ask men (and the few women who owned property) in the city for their signatures. At first they weren't able to get enough people to support their cause, because they had asked for money from a man named Andrew Carnegie, who was famous for giving money to build libraries all over the world. Some of the businessmen in Calgary didn't think Andrew Carnegie was a good man, so they wouldn't sign the petition because of that.

"That didn't deter the women of the literary club. They believed so strongly that Calgary needed a public library that they went out a second time and knocked on doors. This time they got 563 signatures, which was enough

CANADA:
Province of Alberta,
City of Calgary

To the Municipal Council of the City of Calgary:

We, the undersigned resident electors of the said City of Calgary, respectfully pray that a Public Library may be established in this municipality and city under the Public Libraries Act, and pray for the passing of all the necessary By-Laws in the premises.

Calgary, 3rd April, 1908.

[Petition with handwritten signatures]

One page of the 1908 petition to build a library.
Credit: City of Calgary, Corporate Records, Archives, City Clerk's Correspondence, Box 21, Folder 156.

to get the city to agree to build the library. Annie delivered the petition to Calgary's city council in April 1908, and in May a library board was put in place to design and build the new library. The men on the board were some of the most important men in the city, including the mayor, an alderman, and R.B. Bennett, who would later become the prime minister of Canada. Women, like Annie and the literary club members, weren't included on the board, because in those days, very few women held positions of public authority.

"By fall a vote had been held to decide where the new library should go, and construction started at the east end of what was then called Central Park. Andrew Carnegie provided some of the money for the new building and libraries built with 'Carnegie money' often had similar designs, like the wide stairs you see at the front of this library. The company that built the Calgary library decided to use a blueprint that had been made for another Carnegie library in Attleboro, Massachusetts.

"Before the library was even built, the library board hired the chief librarian, a man named Alexander Calhoun. Alexander took care of the purchasing and cataloguing of the books as well as hiring staff for the new library. He believed what Annie and her literary club had believed, that the books in a public library should be for everyone, so he bought books by lots of well-known authors like Shakespeare and Dickens, but he also made sure there were books about plumbing and mechanics and gardening, and other books for people who didn't want to read Shakespeare and Dickens. He also thought there should be lots of books for children, so he hired, Ruth Hopkins, one of the very first children's librarians in the country. Alexander helped to make the Calgary Public Library a place for all people. Annie would have been so happy to see the library she helped create. Sadly, she didn't live to see the result of all her hard work. She became ill and moved to Montreal to be with her daughter, and she died there in 1910.

"The library opened to the public on January 2, 1912, and the first books were borrowed on January 12. People found books by looking them up in a card catalogue; computers hadn't been invented yet.

"Within a few days, all of the 5,200 books the library owned were signed out. Over 3,000 people out of a population of 43,000 people had registered for library cards. To get a library card, you had to have someone in the city sign a letter saying you lived in the city and were a decent person. Kids only needed their parents' permission. If you kept a book for too long, Alexander would send the library's janitor to your house to get it back.

"Just like today, the library wasn't just a place for books. There were reading rooms and places for newspapers, for sure, but there were all kinds of other things going on at the new Central Library. The Calgary Natural History Museum had some space on the top floor for its collections, things like buffalo heads, dinosaur bones, and stuffed birds.

"The Calgary Art Association also had a space in the new library. Calgary didn't have a college yet, so the new Calgary College (which would, many years later, become the University of Calgary) was started in a lecture room on the second floor.

"The library was the heart of the community and lots of people used it. But the library was always a special place for children. They could come and find books, and they could join clubs like the True Blue Girls Club, whose members memorized and recited passages from books. They also came to story times, like the one shown in this photograph.

"Notice that the children are wearing their best clothes for story time. An outing to the library was a very special event. Over the years many people have told library staff stories about their visits to the library. Some of the

Story hour at the library, 1915.
Credit: Calgary Public Library CPL_103-15-01

123

people said that the fancy bathrooms were a highlight for them because they didn't have bathrooms in their houses. Other people have said that they ran up the stairs to see the museum specimens or the statues that were on display. People have said that during bad times, like the Depression, the library was a place where kids could come and sit in front of a fire and read. They loved the library because it was warmer than their houses.

"Children were always important customers in the library, but not all children could get to the library, so librarians used to bring a travelling collection of books to schools. That way, children whose parents couldn't take them to the library could still have books to read. The first school to get a collection was Riverside School.

"Annie and the other members of the Calgary Women's Literary Club were right. The people of Calgary needed and wanted a library, and once they had it, they loved it. The library system grew along with the city. Libraries opened up in communities all over the city. We were lucky that Annie and the women in her book club felt so strongly about a library because now we have one of the busiest library systems in the country. It is still growing, and soon we will have a new Central Library."

The people in the audience clapped as the man finished his story. Sarah and Harry were glad they had come. They loved their library, but until now they hadn't known about its history and the people who worked so hard to get a library for the city. They knew now that it had all started with the dream of Annie Davidson, more than one hundred years ago.

Activities

1. Visit the Memorial Park Library and check out the building and the grounds. Do you see the carvings over the door? Can you find out what the carvings and the other symbols at the front of the library mean?
2. Visit the Calgary Public Library's Community Heritage and Family History Digital Library for pictures of the Memorial Park Library and of Calgary at the time the library was built. See http://calgarylibrary. ca/local-history/.

3. Can you find a picture of the library in Massachusetts that the Calgary Public Library was modelled on? (Hint: It is in Attleboro.)
4. Find out more about Andrew Carnegie. Why did some of the citizens of Calgary object to using his money for a library for their city?
5. Read old newspapers about the opening of the Calgary Public Library. You can see the old papers online at http://www.ourfutureourpast.ca/newspapr/ OR you can see them on microfilm in the Local History Room at the Central Library (616 Macleod Trail SE). What did people think about the new library at the time? Did everyone think it was a good thing?

Further Reading

Brennan, Brian. *The Calgary Public Library: Inspiring Life Stories since 1912*. Calgary: The Calgary Public Library and Kingsley Publishing, 2012

Gorosh, Esther. *Calgary's "Temple of Knowledge": A History of the Calgary Public Library*. Calgary: Century Calgary Publications, 1975.

Sawa, Maureen. *The Library Book: The Story of Libraries from Camels to Computers*. Toronto: Tundra Books, 2006

The merry-go-round that is now at Heritage Park was originally located in Bowness Park.

Credit: Photo illustration by Walt DeBoni

Bowness Booms: John Hextall

Dr. Judith Barge

Sarah and her brother Harry were very excited. Their father was taking them to Bowness Park for a picnic.

"Where is Bowness Park?" asked Harry.

"Bowness Park is on an island in the Bow River at the western end of Bowness," said his father. "There used to be two islands there, but now they are joined together. Bowness itself was once just a hamlet west of Calgary, before it grew to a village and then a town. It became part of The City of Calgary in 1964."

"How will we get there?" asked Sarah. "And how long will it take?"

"We'll take the bus to Bowness," replied Sarah's father. "It should take only about twenty minutes or so. However, it used to take almost three hours to get to Bowness from downtown Calgary by horse and buggy. That was before a bridge was built across the Bow River to shorten the journey."

"Gosh," said Harry. "I'm glad it won't take us three hours. Will we go across that bridge?"

"No," answered Dad. "That bridge is too narrow now to take today's traffic, but you will see it from the bus when we go over the newer Shouldice Bridge that was built alongside it. The old bridge is called the John Hextall Bridge after the man who had it built in 1911. You can still walk or cycle over it."

When everyone was ready, they caught the bus and soon were passing the old John Hextall Bridge.

"Look, there it is," shouted Harry, "and there is a park beside it called John Hextall Park."

"John Hextall must have been an important person," said Sarah. "I wonder who he was."

"Well," said Sarah's father, "John Hextall was an English lawyer who immigrated to Canada in 1908. At that time, Bowness was open cattle ranch land, with only one house called the Bowness Ranch House. However, in 1910, there was a real-estate boom in Calgary, meaning that there were lots of houses being built and house prices were going up. Mr. Hextall decided to buy all the ranch land at Bowness, and he and his family moved into the ranch house. Then he thought it would be a good idea to

John Hextall
Credit: Bowness Historical Society

divide his land into lots to sell to people wanting to build a house at Bowness. He called his building plan Bowness Estates. All the houses had to be built to very high standards, were on large lots, and were quite expensive.

"That was when he decided to build his bridge across the Bow River," continued Sarah's father, "but you could only go across it if you had special

The Hextall family at their Bowness Ranch, about 1911.
Credit: Bowness Historical Society

permission from Mr. Hextall. Back then there were no buses and people travelled by streetcars that ran on rails, a bit like an old-fashioned CTrain service but much slower and usually only one or two streetcars at a time. Mr. Hextall wanted to get the streetcar service for Bowness so he had to think of a way to achieve this. He decided to give his bridge to The City of Calgary, along with two river islands at the western end of his property, in exchange for streetcar service to Bowness. The river islands were to be used for a park that he named Bowness Park. So, thanks to John Hextall, from 1912, hundreds of Calgarians began to ride over the John Hextall Bridge on the Bowness streetcar, to spend a wonderful day at beautiful Bowness Park."

A street car going over the Hextall Bridge on the Bow River, about 1914.
Credit: Bowness Historical Society

Sarah was gazing out of the bus window as they passed through Bowness. Suddenly, she asked, "Did John Hextall build all these houses then?"

"No, he didn't," said Sarah's father. "He only got to build a handful of very nice homes before the First World War broke out in 1914. The war changed the way Canadians earned and spent their money, and people were no longer as eager to build and buy houses. Also, Mr. Hextall was in poor health, and he died the same year. In fact, very few people lived at Bowness until it became a village in 1948. There were so few houses that some of the ranch land at Bowness was used as a flying field for early aeroplanes between

1919 and 1928. You could pay to take short aeroplane rides, but there were quite a few crash landings because the ground was so rough.

"However, Mr. Hextall did manage to build himself a large mansion at the far western end of his property," continued her father. "It had a grand entrance hall, a library, and a ballroom. He also built a Golf and Country Club house on a hill overlooking Bowness."

"Can we see his mansion?" asked Harry.

The Hextall mansion, about 1913.
Credit: Bowness Historical Society

"I'm afraid not," said his father. "After Mr. Hextall died, his house was sold to pay off his debts. In 1926 it became part of the Wood's Christian Home, which was a home for orphaned children. Unfortunately there was a small fire in the house in 1975, and it was torn down. It was replaced recently by a new building at Wood's Christian Home. Also, the Golf and Country Club met a similar fate when it was destroyed by fire in 1997. However, I could take you on the tour of the Hextall homes that Bowness Historical Society runs during Historic Calgary Week. The homes have quite distinctive architecture, and you even get to go inside some of them. In fact, we will be passing two of them in a minute on the right, as we are almost at the park now."

On their way into Bowness Park, Harry and Sarah's father pointed out where the Bowness Ranch House used to be situated, just to the west of the park entrance. He also told the children that before the river islands became a park, cattle were kept there, and there were barns and corrals where the teahouse and tables are now.

"Where should we have our picnic?" asked Sarah.

"I think we will find a nice, shady spot near the playground," replied Sarah's father. "Then you can play for a while before we eat."

Sarah and Harry had a terrific time at the new playground that was built when the park was redeveloped in 2014. They especially liked the rope tower that spun around, and the flying saucer swings that you can lie down on. By the time they had finished playing, they were very hungry and thirsty and enjoyed their sandwiches, cake, and lemonade.

After lunch they all took a short walk along the pretty creek path. They saw dogwoods, silver-berry, willows, and wild roses, lots of birds, and a few squirrels. They admired the beautiful trees, and their father pointed out the Douglas fir trees. He told them that the First Nations used to camp by the river and make their bows from the Douglas fir wood.

"Is that why the river is called the Bow River?" asked Sarah.

"Very likely," answered her father.

"Can you camp in the park," asked Harry.

"No. But between the 1920s and the 1940s you could. You could also rent one of eight tiny cottages for a week, a month, or for the whole summer."

"Wow," said Harry, "that must have been fun!"

"What should we do next?" piped up Sarah.

"Would you like to go boating on the lagoon?" asked their father.

"Yippee!" Sarah and Harry both cried.

Out on the lagoon, paddling a large canoe, they all laughed when they got a bit too close to the fountain and got sprayed. Their father told them that there used to be a fountain in the lagoon that changed colour. He also told them about something called an "orthophonic" that used to be in the middle of the lagoon. "It looked like a square, wooden tower with loudspeakers on three sides, and it played music," he said.

"How did it work?" asked Sarah.

"Well, inside there was a sort of record player," explained Dad, "and someone had to go out to it by boat and climb inside it to play the records."

After they took their boat back to the boat house, they went for a short ride on the miniature train.

"That was great," said Harry. "Are there any more rides in the park?"

"There used to be quite a lot of rides, including a Ferris wheel and a merry-go-round," replied their father. "They were getting old and weren't used as much, so they were removed. The merry-go-round was moved to Heritage Park where you can still ride it today."

Dad told them that there used to be a dance pavilion where bands played live music in the evenings. He also told them about the big swimming pools that used to be in the park.

"Where were the pools?" asked Sarah.

"They were built in 1914 at the east end of the park," Dad said. "They had diving boards, a water slide, and changing rooms. They were closed a long time ago."

"Please may we get an ice-cream from the snack bar?" asked Harry.

"Yes, you can, but after that I'm afraid it is time to go home."

"Can we come back again?" asked Sarah.

"Certainly," Dad said. "We can also come back in the winter to skate on the lagoon."

Streetcars taking people to Freeze's annual picnic at Bowness Park.
Credit: Bowness Historical Society

"Hooray!" cried Sarah and Harry.

As they waited for the bus to take them home again, everyone agreed that they had all had a wonderful day out at Bowness Park. Sarah and Harry had also learned a lot about John Hextall and the history of early Bowness.

Activities

1. Visit Heritage Park and ride the streetcar from the car park to take you to the entrance. Look for the merry-go-round that used to be in Bowness Park and take a ride.

2. Visit Bowness Park and look for all the special signs that tell you about the history of the park. Find the answers to the following questions:

    a. When were the Bowness Ranch buildings removed from the park?

    b. From where did the people who rented the cottages in the park get their water?

    c. When did buses replace streetcars?

    d. Why were the swimming pools closed for a season in 1952?

    e. When was the orthophonic on the lagoon replaced with a loudspeaker system?

    f. How many rides did Funland have? Can you name some of them?

3. Ask someone to take you on the Bowness Historical Society's tour of the Hextall houses during Historic Calgary Week, normally held from the last week of July into the first week of August.

4. Go to the Calgary Public Library and find two books published by the Bowness Historical Society: *Bowness: Our Village in the Valley* and *Bowness: Past and Present 1911-2011*. Your school library may also have copies of these books. Look carefully at the photographs to see how Bowness and Bowness Park have changed over the years. With the help of these books, draw or paint a picture of something connected with the history of early Bowness. Here are some ideas: a streetcar, the John Hextall Bridge, Bowness Park, the Bowness Ranch House, the Hextall mansion, or one of the Hextall houses.

Captain Fred McCall and Captain Wilfred "Wop" May were featured aviators at the 1919 Calgary Exhibition. This was the second year that the Stampede was held jointly with the Calgary Exhibition. The end of World War I was being celebrated.
Credit: Courtesy of the Calgary Stampede Archives

The Aviation Adventures of
Fearless Freddie McCall

Shirlee Smith Matheson

The tail of a big yellow airplane jutted out from the War and the Home Front display in the Glenbow Museum's *Mavericks: An Incorrigible History of Alberta* exhibition, demanding visitors' attention. Harry and Sarah quickly stepped from the elevator, followed by the Glenbow guide – whose name-tag read Colleen – and raced over to learn the story behind this exciting display.

Who flew this open-cockpit, bi-wing airplane? What was his story?

The lighted display, showcasing a handsome young man with a twinkle in his eyes, answers this question. He is World War One Flying Ace, Captain Freddie McCall, DSO, DFC, MC and Bar.

"Is this pilot the reason the Calgary Municipal Airport was named McCall Field?" Sarah asked.

"And is McCall Lake Golf Course on McKnight Boulevard in northeast Calgary also named for him?" Harry asked.

"And a new shopping centre by the airport, McCall Landing?" Sarah added.

"You two already know a lot about Calgary's landmarks!" Colleen noted with a smile. "To add another place name to your list, there is also an electoral district, Calgary-McCall. Yes, the McCall name does have an exciting history, but to really understand its importance to Calgary's – and Canada's – past, we must become airborne. Let's pretend we're taking a flight in the Jenny."

"This airplane is called Jenny?" Sarah inquired.

"Yes. This is a trainer aircraft, a Curtiss JN-4, nicknamed the 'Jenny.' It was built by the Curtiss Aeroplane Company of New York. The Jenny worked hard to help pilots learn how to fly for their life-or-death missions in the First World War. After the war, these aircraft were sold to private owners for barnstorming. Stunt-pilots would fly them, individually or in groups called 'flying circuses,' to different towns to perform tricks in the air – loops and dives and pretend dog-fights – or they would take people up for rides."

Fred McCall's "Jenny" airplane in 1919.
Credit: Glenbow Archives NB-16-418

"Let's fly!" Harry exclaimed.

"Okay. Let's say that Harry is in the front open cockpit."

"Yeah! I'm the pilot," Harry said.

"Not so fast," Colleen laughed. "The pilot sits in the rear cockpit and the passengers in front."

"Oh," Harry said, sounding rather disappointed.

"But, we can take turns," Sarah offered. "Let's find out how Captain Freddie learned to fly."

Sarah and Harry quickly read the information on the lighted displays to

136

learn that Freddie McCall was born in Vernon, British Columbia, and grew up in Calgary. When the First World War broke out, Freddie signed up to help fight for our freedom. He was accepted for service in the 175th Overseas Battalion of the Canadian Expeditionary Force (the army) and bravely embarked on a trip that guaranteed no return ticket.

"That's scary!" Sarah exclaimed.

"You have to be brave when you're going to war," Harry said. "I would be, too."

Sarah and Colleen smiled as they continued to learn more about Freddie's war experiences.

"Once overseas, in England, McCall quickly re-mustered to join the Royal Flying Corp (RFC) so he could learn to fly," Colleen said.

Another display sign stated that Freddie McCall had just celebrated his twenty-second birthday on December 4, 1917, when he was sent to France. But most shocking was the news that he had been given only one hour and forty minutes of flight training in the air before he was sent out to find and fight enemy aircraft!

"Wow! That's not very much time!" Sarah exclaimed. "He must have been really smart!"

"And fearless," Harry added.

"I like that," Sarah said. "His warrior name could be Fearless Freddie McCall!"

"That's a perfect name," Colleen agreed. "But the reason he had so little training was because the war was raging in Europe, and pilots were needed right away.

"Freddie wasn't a large man," Collen continued. "In fact he was about the same height as me, 5 feet 6 inches, or 168 centimetres, and he weighed just 140 pounds, or 64 kilograms."

"Same as you?" Sarah asked.

"Just about," Colleen smiled.

"Wow, I bet I'll be lots bigger than that when I grow up!" Harry boasted.

"You might be, but Freddie's small size proved to be a real asset in getting in and out of the tight cockpits, as well as being quick when turning, sighting, and pursuing enemy aircraft."

The first airplane that Fred McCall flew in combat was the RE-8, an airplane designed for reconnaissance and not for aerial combat.
Credit: Glenbow Archives NA-4671-22

"And look," Sarah said. "It says that Captain Freddie was first given a slow airplane called an RE-8, not a real fighter plane."

"Yes. His first airplane in the war was an open-cockpit, two-seater, Reconnaissance Experimental airplane called an RE-8," Colleen noted. "And look here: it tells us that just before Freddie was assigned to his RE-8 that an entire patrol of RE-8s had been involved in an aerial dogfight against the famous enemy pilot The Red Baron and his 'Flying Circus.' Not one of those six Allied aircraft returned from that fight, and only two crew members had survived."

"Freddie must have been a super good pilot!" Sarah exclaimed. "Just look at these pictures! The sky is filled with airplanes dashing this way and that, flying above and below enemy aircraft."

"Those are called aerial dogfights," Harry said, "and you can sure see why!"

"Yes, Freddie's flights were fast and furious," Colleen agreed. "He had to work hard and be really skillful to keep that clumsy, cloth-covered RE-8 in the air and out of the enemy's range. And look at the gun he had to aim and fire! It was called a Lewis machine gun. See this diagram where it shows how the firing mechanism was synchronized so the bullets shot cleanly between the whirling propeller blades? He had all this to deal with, in an aircraft meant mainly for reconnaissance, or viewing and photographing the action below. He had to watch for movements and flashes of enemy guns, and exploding bombs. Also, there were maybe seventy aircraft in the air at once, taking part in those furious dogfights."

"Wow!" was the only response the children could make to this display of bravery and action.

Sarah stopped to read a sign that said in 1918 the Royal Flying Corps was renamed the Royal Air Force (RAF), but Harry was more interested in looking at the model of the new, fast fighter airplane that Freddie was assigned next: an SE-5A.

"Look, this single-seat airplane had two guns!" he exclaimed. "A Vickers machine gun up here on the top left side of the fuselage – that must mean the main body of the airplane – and a Lewis gun above the centre section of the upper wing. Like, wow! One guy all by himself, flying the plane, and at the same time aiming *two* guns!"

"Not many were as successful as Freddie McCall," Colleen said. "Sadly, some never returned home, but Captain Freddie McCall came back home to Calgary, welcomed and decorated as a hero. He was Canada's fifth-ranking air ace and was awarded the Distinguished Service Order, the Military Cross, twice, and the Distinguished Flying Cross. He was indeed an outstanding pilot with extraordinary flying skills."

"What did he do when he came back?" Sarah asked. "Did he fly here, too?"

"I'll bet he did!" Harry said. "You wouldn't keep Captain Freddie out of the air!" He pointed to the photos of Freddie with another handsome pilot, from Edmonton, named "Wop" May.

"See, I knew it!" Harry said excitedly, as he learned that on returning to Alberta from the war, Freddie and Wilfred "Wop" May paid $500 each for two Curtiss JN-4D Jennies.

"After they bought the planes, they barnstormed around Calgary and to small towns in southern Alberta, showing off their amazing flying skills to thousands of people who had never seen an airplane," Colleen said, "They would land in farmers' fields, and charge people a penny a pound to go up for rides."

"Gee, that would be cheap for me!" Harry said. "And even cheaper for you, Sarah!"

"Yes, you could likely pay for a ride just with your allowance!" Colleen laughed. "See here, one of the Jennies had a griffon emblem painted on the fuselage and the other a First Nations chief with feather headdress."

"Just like the one in front of us," Sarah said. "I knew Freddie would choose the chief."

"Well, actually, he did start with the chief, but as you'll see in this photo, that plane became involved – and subsequently was wrecked – in a very

The crash landing by Fred McCall of his "Jenny" on top of the carousel at the 1919 Calgary Exhibition.
Credit: Glenbow Archives NA-1451-27

famous forced landing. In fact it was featured in a 'Ripley's Believe it or Not' column and called 'The Most Famous Forced Landing in the World'! After that, he flew the 'griffon' Jenny," Colleen said. "Just look at this picture."

"Can it be true?" Harry asked, amazed. "He landed right on top of a merry-go-round!"

"It happened at the Calgary Exhibition – we call it the Calgary Stampede, now – in 1919. He had two young boys as passengers. As you now know, these two passengers were riding in the front cockpit, when his engine quit right after he'd taken-off from the infield. He couldn't get back there because there was a race going on; and he couldn't land on the midway because hundreds of people would be hit and maybe killed. So he looked down at the canvas top of the merry-go-round and made this amazing forced landing. You can't see it in this photograph, but the pole on top of the merry-go-round pierced right between the seats of the two boys in the front cockpit."

"Were they hurt, or… killed?" Sarah quietly asked.

"Amazingly no one was injured," Colleen reassured her, "but the Jenny was a write-off. So, he took over flying the other Jenny, the one with the griffon painted on its side. 'Wop' May went on from barnstorming to flying in northern Alberta. In fact the North West Mounted Police hired him to guide the first aerial search ever used to track down a fugitive, the famous 'Mad Trapper.' But, that's another story!"

"What did Freddie do after 'Wop' left for the North?" Harry asked.

"Freddie continued pioneering aviation in southern Alberta, organizing flying clubs and starting up new airlines," Colleen said. "But, he did it with such flair. He was a real character!"

"Tell us some of his adventures here in Calgary," Harry pleaded. "I *like* this guy!"

Colleen laughed and continued telling stories to her delighted audience. "Well, he wanted people to learn to fly, so in the summer of 1919 he founded the Calgary Aero Club, now called the Calgary Flying Club, which is located out at Springbank Airport. Their first annual general meeting was held in the Crystal Ballroom of the Palliser Hotel."

"Pretty fancy!" Sarah said.

"Yes, it was," Colleen said, emphasizing the word "was."

"What do you mean?" Harry asked, his interest piqued.

"Well, Freddie decided that the people attending the meeting would be excited to see a real airplane up close, so he and a crew brought the club's Cirrus Moth up in the freight elevator."

"Wasn't it too big?" Harry asked.

"The wings on this airplane folded in, and they also removed the propeller, but even then they had to bring it up the elevator on its nose. And that's where the trouble started."

Eyes sparkling, Harry and Sarah glanced at one another, anticipating another good story.

"They set the airplane up on a stage behind the head table, unfolded the wings, and reattached the propeller. Everything was going fine, and people were totally impressed. But that wasn't enough for our famous Freddie McCall. These folks deserved the real thing! He jumped into the cockpit and called for a helper to spin the prop. It sputtered and died. When he tried it again, the same thing happened. Freddie kept adding more throttle. The engine suddenly caught and roared to life, and out burst a cloud of intense blue smoke that completely filled the room!"

"How did that happen?" Sarah asked.

"Apparently, oil had run into the cylinders when the aircraft was tipped up for its ride on the elevator," Colleen explained. "The result was an intense and choking stench that drove everyone to the door and left the Crystal Ballroom with black walls and ruined draperies."

Harry and Sarah couldn't help but giggle at the image of people in fancy dress racing from the room and out the door of the hotel.

"Tell us more!" Harry exclaimed. He touched the video display to see a photo of a Stinson Detroiter, the first aircraft Freddie flew that had a roof. And it was painted purple. "A purple airplane! What's the story on this one?"

"Well, in March of 1928, Freddie became the chief pilot for Purple Label Airlines, and so the airplane was painted purple. When that company became

A Stinson Detroiter airplane, the first one that Fred McCall flew that had a closed in cockpit.
Credit: Glenbow Archives NA-5120-1

Great Western Airways, Freddie again was hired as general manager and chief pilot. He was the first pilot ever to fly in to Banff, on January 19, 1929, landing on the ice of the Bow River. And it was in this Stinson Detroiter, a few weeks later, that he also took on a job that could have resulted in a real disaster."

The guide paused to allow the children to examine photographs of the airplane being unloaded with wooden boxes holding some kind of cargo.

"An oil company planned to 'shoot' its drilling wells at Turner Valley, using a very explosive substance called nitroglycerine, to help make the well produce oil," Colleen said in a lowered voice. "This material was too dangerous to be transported by rail or road, and so Freddie was hired to fly to Montana to pick it up. He would be flying 250 miles – that's about four hundred kilometres – each way in sub-zero temperatures, to pick up 100 quart containers (a quart is about the same size as a litre) of nitro, packed in rubber-covered cases, along with a dozen sticks of dynamite, which he shoved under the seat."

The children could barely breathe as they took in the enormous danger of such a trip.

"But he didn't blow up!" Harry said. "How did he do it, and get back safely?"

143

Transferring nitroglycerine and dynamite from Fred McCall's airplane after he landed in Calgary.
Credit: Glenbow Archives PA-3682-42

"Well, he was lucky! Strong headwinds on the return trip meant the plane used much more fuel than they'd expected, and when he landed at the frozen airstrip on Banff Coach Road, his fuel gauge read below empty. The Stinson bounced twice as it hit the frozen surface, and then it skidded to a stop, completely out of fuel. Freddie stepped out of the aircraft. He was a brave man and had taken a lot of risks in his flying career, but even he freaked out when he saw one of the crew begin to unload a case *while smoking*! That was just too risky for the daring pilot, Freddie McCall!" Colleen laughed. "He immediately ordered the man to get away from the airplane and put out his cigarette."

"Is there a book I could read about Freddie McCall?" asked Sarah. "I'd like to know more about him."

"There is indeed *so much* more." Colleen said. "When he came home from the war, Freddie married a lovely lady named Genevieve, and they had two children, Gerrie and Fred. When the Second World War broke out in 1939, Freddie served with the RCAF, and he retired as a Squadron Leader.

A photo of Genevieve McCall, Freddie McCall's wife.

He was inducted into Canada's Aviation Hall of Fame for his accomplishments as a wartime pilot and pioneer aviator in Alberta.

"Unfortunately, he died quite young, when he was only fifty-three, on January 22, 1949. But as you can see here, his legend lives on, through his awards. He has given his name to places like the airport, the golf course, and an electoral district. This *Mavericks: An Incorrigible History of Alberta* exhibit also honours him, as does a book titled *Maverick in the Sky: The Aerial Adventures of WWI Flying Ace Freddie McCall*, by Calgary author Shirlee Smith Matheson. This book contains many more wonderful stories about Freddie."

"That's great, I'll read it, too," Harry said. "But, how did this Jenny display get here to the Glenbow?"

"When the McCalls' son Fred grew up, he also pursued a career in the Canadian military. He was inducted as an Officer in the Order of Military Merit, OMM, and he was awarded the Canadian Forces Decoration, CD, for his service. When he retired, he became a volunteer with the Calgary Aero Space Museum. He worked on projects restoring old planes and got the idea that a Curtiss Jenny should be built for display. This was an airplane that was used to pioneer aviation in Calgary and southern Alberta, and he thought it deserved a place in an aviation museum.

"At this point the Glenbow Museum contacted Shirlee Matheson, the author I was talking about, who also worked at the Aero Space Museum. They asked her to do some research on the amazing life of Captain Freddie McCall so he could be included in the *Mavericks* exhibit. Shirlee told them that Freddie's son Fred and a team of aircraft restorers were building a replica of Captain Freddie's Jenny. Of course, the Glenbow Museum wanted to include the finished aircraft in its new exhibition. But, because of its size, the Jenny had to be displayed with only two wings attached, with the other two being displayed separately as you can see, up on the wall."

Harry and Sarah continued to admire the big, yellow aircraft as the story came to its end.

Colleen smiled. "Now is there anything else you'd like to know about the intrepid Freddie McCall?"

"I want to learn *lots* more about him, and other pilots who pioneered flying in Calgary," Harry said. "I've seen pictures of air shows where airplanes are flying all over and doing super stunts. In fact, I think I'd like to become a pilot some day."

"There are several flying schools right here in our city, and at nearby airstrips," Colleen said. "That's quite a good plan – for boys and for girls," she added, nodding toward Sarah.

"I don't know if I'd want to be a pilot," Sarah said, "but aren't there other things one can do that are connected with airplanes?"

"Definitely," Colleen said. "One could become an engineer – fixing or even designing airframe, electrical, or mechanical systems; or you could work with a flying company in an office, or in air-traffic control, airport management, customer services, baggage handling – there are all kinds of jobs that are related to planes. You could also write about airplanes and aviation history.

"As you can see, stories live forever."

Activities

1. Go to the Glenbow Museum, in Calgary, Alberta, and walk through the *Mavericks: An Incorrigible History of Alberta* exhibit.
2. Take a trip to the Aero Space Museum, Calgary, Alberta, and visit a display in the hangar about Freddie McCall, Wop May, and other Alberta aviation pioneers.

3. Go to the Military Museums in Calgary, Alberta, and check out their Air Force Gallery display, which has a life-size mannequin of Freddie McCall in his original uniform and medals.

4. Read *Maverick in the Sky: The Aerial Adventures of WWI Flying Ace Freddie McCall* by Shirlee Smith Matheson (Calgary: Frontenac House, 2010).

A replica of Nellie McClung's Calgary house in Heritage Park. The original house still stands on Fourteenth Avenue SW.
Credit: Walt DeBoni

Nellie McClung
and the Famous Five

Faye Reineberg Holt

Last year, Sarah's class visited the Glenbow Museum. The guide had encouraged the class to stop at the nearby Famous Five statues. Sarah studied the statues while her friend snapped selfies. Why, she wondered, were these five women famous? They weren't musicians, actors, or sports heroes.

This year, her new teacher planned a visit to the Famous Five Centre at Heritage Park.

"Nellie McClung and four other women wanted women in Canada to have the same rights as men," her teacher said.

When Sarah mentioned the field trip to her mom, the reaction surprised her. "I can't go that day, but Grandma might want to volunteer."

Grandma was sitting on the couch beside Harry, who was playing a video game. "Of course. How exciting!" she said, adding, "Nellie McClung was a famous writer and speaker in my mother's time."

Mom looked at Sarah. "I wish Harry could go, too."

"Grandma can come but not Harry," replied Sarah. She loved her brother, but it was a terrible idea.

At mention of his name, Harry looked up. "What can't I do?" he asked.

"Come with my class. Not that you would care. It's about women."

"Both you and Harry should learn about Nellie McClung," said Mom. "She and others helped to create a country where women have the right to vote and do anything men can do."

Grandma added, "My mother and I have always voted. But my grandmother had no say in government."

Harry went back to his game. Sarah, Mom, and Grandma continued talking about women in the old days. To prepare for the Heritage Park trip, the teacher had given homework. The assignment read, "Research Nellie McClung, and then write a page about this famous Canadian."

"Sarah, your great-grandma – my mom – was born in 1929. That same year, women were finally declared to be persons," Grandma said. "Before that, they raised their children and worked hard, but they weren't guaranteed more legal rights than children."

How dumb, thought Sarah.

Grandma wanted to tell more stories. But, impatient, Sarah went on the computer. Her assignment seemed hard. There was just too much information.

For the October day of the field trip, the weather was perfect. Bright and early, Grandma appeared on their doorstep.

"I hope the guide talks about Nellie being a famous writer," she noted cheerfully to Mom. "Remember me reading *Sowing Seeds in Danny* to you when you were a girl?"

Mom nodded. "I loved it."

"That book was a bestseller. So Mrs. McClung was invited to read and talk to her fans. Emily Murphy was a writer and cared about women's rights and problems, too. They became great friends."

Sarah liked writing. Sometimes, she thought she wanted to be a writer. Other times, she dreamed of being a science teacher or artist. The possibilities were endless.

The day of the field trip, they piled into the car. At school, the class boarded a bus. After it pulled into Heritage Park, they wandered down to the McClung house. They didn't go up the grand steps to the verandah but entered by a lower door. There, they hung backpacks and jackets on hooks. Almost immediately, they were taken upstairs to what the guide called the parlour.

"Children, please sit on the green carpet. Adults can sit in the chairs."

Sarah was glad. If Grandma sat on the floor, they would have to struggle to help her stand up. The house had a chandelier, dark wood, and lace curtains. The piano and old furniture made her wonder about the old days.

Nellie McClung at her desk, about 1908-1910.
Credit: Glenbow Archives NA-1514-3

"Welcome," added the guide. "I'll be sharing stories about Nellie McClung and the Famous Five. But first, notice how I am dressed. This would be how women in the 1920s dressed. That was when Nellie McClung lived in a Calgary home very like this one. Now, who can tell me about Mrs. McClung and the Famous Five?"

Grandma didn't raise her hand, but Sarah did.

"Mrs. McClung was a writer and made speeches about women having the right to vote."

"Yes. She wrote nine fiction books and eight nonfiction books." The guide talked and asked questions. "Our Nell, as many called her, was born in Chatsworth, Ontario, in 1873. That was just six years after Canadian Confederation. When she was young, her parents moved to a homestead in Manitoba. So, Nellie didn't go to school until she was almost your age."

Sarah couldn't imagine not going to school.

"When she was growing up, it was considered improper for girls to run in races or play games like baseball. Nellie knew she could do those things as well as boys – if given a chance. Then, when she became a teacher in a one-room school, she encouraged boys and girls to do the same things and play the same games."

Teaching in a one room school must have been strange, Sarah thought.

"After she married Wesley McClung, a pharmacist, they moved to

Winnipeg. There, she blossomed as a writer and became a great speaker. She wanted to make sure girls and women had the same rights as boys and men. Sometimes, her audiences roared with laughter. Other times, she made them want to march down the streets in protest. Now, do any of you enjoy being in plays?"

Sarah's hand shot up.

"So did Mrs. McClung," said the guide. "Just like today, provinces made some laws. The Canadian government made other ones. In one play, she pretended to be the premier of Manitoba. She used his own speeches but changed the words. She gave reasons why men should not be allowed to vote. The premier was embarrassed. By 1915 the McClung family moved to Edmonton. Yet, due to her influence, in January 1916, Manitoba became the first province in Canada to grant women the right to vote. In March Saskatchewan women could vote. In Alberta –"

A boy's hand went up.

"Yes?" asked the guide.

"Any of us could write, act in plays, or lecture people." It was Alec, one of the smartest boys in the class. "That doesn't make us famous."

The class groaned. Alec smiled. Strangely, he even liked his nickname, Smart Aleck, even though it wasn't meant as a compliment.

Fortunately, the guide simply continued, "I was getting to that. A good friend, Emily Murphy, also lived in Edmonton. Together, they pushed for women's rights. In April 1916, the law changed, allowing Alberta women to vote and run in provincial elections."

"But –" Alec started.

"Remember your manners," their teacher said. She stared at Alec.

"That very year, two women were elected to the Alberta Legislature. Many women wanted prohibition, too, and it was made the law."

"What is prohibition?" a classmate asked.

"A law to make buying or selling alcohol illegal. It was a bit like today's laws against drugs. That same year, Emily Murphy was appointed the first woman police magistrate in the British Empire. Isn't that amazing?"

Everyone nodded except Alec.

"So, what is a magistrate?" Alec asked.

"It is a job very like being a judge. In fact, often, Emily was said to be the first woman judge in the British Empire. However, while she had the power to hear cases about women and children, she couldn't act as the judge in many serious criminal cases." The guide continued, "Even when she was hearing cases about women and children, one lawyer, Mr. Jackson, made her job difficult."

Sarah and her classmates looked at Alec.

The procession as Lord Chancellor John Sankey is about to deliver the decision of the British Imperial Privy Council confirming that women are indeed persons.
Credit: Glenbow Archives NA-4953-1

"Mr. Jackson had a case in Emily's courtroom. He objected to her being the magistrate. He said that, according to Canadian law, women were classified with children and people who had mental illness."

"You mean insane people?" offered Alec.

"That was the language of the time. In any case, Emily noted his objection. Then, she went on with the case. He did the same thing again and again. Finally, Emily consulted her brothers who were Ontario lawyers. Do any of you have brothers who help when you have difficulties?"

Sarah thought about the time Harry stuck up for her when she was being bullied.

The guide continued, "Emily's brothers said that, in Canada's Constitution, the pronoun 'he' was used. So, for example, only men could be appointed to the Senate. Also, that might mean women couldn't hold other such offices, too. Well, it began a thirteen-year legal fight for Emily. Now, how many of you would have given up?"

Some put up their hands but not Sarah.

"In the meantime, Nellie McClung was elected to Alberta's Legislature. Then, in 1923, she and her family moved to Calgary. However, she was still a Member of the Legislature, and she served until 1926."

The guide directed them into the dining room. There, beautiful china plates decorated the ledges around the walls.

"Here women would have Pink Teas. They arrived at Nellie's door wearing something pink. Most men were uncomfortable at the teas and didn't attend. As a result, the women could talk openly about their rights and concerns."

"Pink wouldn't keep me away," mumbled Alec.

Somehow, Sarah felt herself stepping back in time. She imagined being Nellie. She might use the large, strange-looking telephone to invite women to tea. She and other women would wear long dresses, elegant hats, and white gloves. They would eat fancy sandwiches or squares and talk about important ideas.

As Nellie, she would say, "My Edmonton friend, Emily Murphy, wants this persons problem settled. Yes, we must prove the Canadian Constitution doesn't forbid our being made senators." Sarah was surprised by how much she remembered. If she needed to, maybe she could make speeches, too.

"Sarah," Grandma whispered. Standing nearby, perhaps she had noticed that Sarah was daydreaming.

"Let's go upstairs," said the guide.

Upstairs were bedrooms. Two were for the three children and one for Nellie and her husband. There, the white bedspread was lacy, and the two pillow cases had writing on them.

"Embroidery done by Nellie," the guide said. "Will someone read the words on the pillow cases?"

This time Sarah was chosen.

"I slept and dreamed that life was beauty," Sarah read. "I woke and found that life was duty."

Grandma nodded in approval.

"Our Nell believed people must stand up for what they believe." On the opposite wall, a huge poster showed portraits of the women. "They are the Famous Five!"

A composite of five photographs of the Famous Five. They are, clockwise from the lower left, Louise McKinney, Irene Parlby, Emily Murphy, Henrietta Muir Edwards, and Nellie McClung.
Credit: Famous Five Foundation

She pointed out Nellie and Emily. Then, she spoke about the other three who signed Emily's petition. "From the Fort Macleod area, Henrietta Edwards wrote about laws for Alberta women and was president of a Canadian women's group. From Claresholm, Louise McKinney worked with the Women's Christian Temperance Union for prohibition. She was elected to Alberta's Legislature in 1917 as one of the first two women in Alberta and in the British Empire."

Grandma looked spellbound.

"Irene Parlby married a farmer from Alix, Alberta," added the guide. "She became a leader for farm women. In 1923 she was elected to the Legislature, too. Then, she was appointed as our first woman cabinet minister. Aren't these amazing women?

"They did not just sign one petition and the fight ended," added the guide. "Before they could claim victory, Alberta and Canada's courts ruled against them. Legally, any five interested Canadians could protest a court decision to the Privy Council in England. At that time, it was the final word on Canada's laws. The women sent their petition. It was named the Persons Case. In October 1929, the Privy Council ruled. In Canada, women were persons entitled to the same rights and privileges as men."

"Humans are always persons! But I guess the women deserve to be famous, too." Finally, Alec had said something everyone supported.

The guide passed around

The Canadian stamp issued in 1973 on the 100th anniversary of Nellie McClung's birth.

Credit: Canada Post

A statue of Nellie McClung as part of the Famous Five exhibit that was unveiled on October 18, 1999 at Olympic Plaza in Calgary. A similar exhibit was erected one year later on Parliament Hill in Ottawa.
Credit: Faye Reineberg Holt

black and white pictures. Also, she showed a copy of Nellie's handwritten notebook. "These women loved their children," she added. "As mothers, they were responsible for their children. They wanted to help make good decisions for their children, province, and country."

"Grandma," Sarah said on the way home. "I think Harry needs to learn about the Famous Five, too."

Grandma agreed. "Maybe he will be inspired to make a difference in the world, just as we have been today."

Activities

1. Draft Sarah's assignment about Nellie McClung. Using the Internet, go to the Glenbow Archives, and using the link to photographs, find two that you like. Click on each and print the sheet that shows the photo and gives information about it. Add the two copies to your assignment.

2. Write a paragraph or give a presentation at school explaining what you think would have been most important to Sarah in her visit to the Famous Five House.

3. Compare childhood in the past with childhood today.

4. Pretend it is 1915. Plan an afternoon of speeches, debates, or plays about issues important to the Famous Five. An important one would be provincial and national votes for women, or post-secondary and professional education for women.

Further Reading

Kids' Books

Bentham, Mary Lile. *Nellie McClung*. Toronto: Fitzhenry & Whiteside, 2000.

Crook, Connie Brummel. *Nellie's Quest*. Toronto: Fitzhenry & Whiteside, 1998.

Crook, Connie Brummel. *Nellie's Victory*. Toronto: Fitzhenry & Whiteside, 1999.

Dawson, Willow. *Hyena in Petticoats: The Story of Suffragette Nellie*

McClung. Toronto: Penguin Canada, 2011; Toronto: Kids Can Press, 2010.

Macleod, Elizabeth. *The Kids Book of Great Canadian Women*. Toronto: Kids Can Press, 2006.

Macpherson, Margaret. *Nellie McClung*. Toronto: Dundurn, 2003.

Pezzi, Bryan. *Nellie McClung*. Calgary: Weigl Educational Publishers, 2007.

Adults' Books

McClung, Nellie. *Clearing in the West*. Toronto: Thomas Allen and Son, Ltd., 1935. (Reprinted by Athabasca University Press, 1992.)

McClung, Nellie. *Purple Springs*. Toronto: Thomas Allen and Son, Ltd., 1921. (Reprinted by University of Toronto Press, 1992.)

Rasmussen, Linda, Lorna Rasmussen, Candace Savage, and Anne Wheeler, eds. *A Harvest Yet to Reap*. Toronto: Canadian Women's Press, 1976.

Savage, Candace. *Our Nell*. Saskatoon: Western Producer Prairie Books, 1979.

Millar, Nancy. *Famous Five: Five Canadian Women and Their Fight to Become Persons*. Calgary: Deadwood Publishing, 2003.

About The Authors

Barge, Dr. Judith. Judith is a former teacher and historic sites consultant, and presently volunteers as a member of the Board of Directors of Bowness Historical Society. For the past 12 years she has given tours of the Hextall Homes during Historic Calgary Week.

DeBoni, Irene. A retired teacher, Irene lives in Eau Claire not far from where the Prince family once lived and knows the area around the 1886 Café very well. She has been on the planning committee for Historic Calgary Week for many years. Irene gives tours of Calgary's downtown area during the summer months as part of the Transalta retirees group.

DeBoni, Walt. A retired executive, Walt has also been involved with Historic Calgary Week for many years. He is thrilled when his passion for history and photography coincide.

Gross, Cory. Cory is the owner of Sandstone Prehistoric Safaris Calgary, which offers earth science-based tours and programs in the Calgary Area. He also works full-time as a school programs educator at the Glenbow Museum and part-time as an interpreter at the Calgary Zoo.

Hayes, Christine. A native Calgarian, Christine has been a reference assistant with the Humanities and Community Heritage and Family History collection for over 10 years, specializing in genealogical research and local history. One of her recent projects was assisting author Brian Brennan with his research on the centennial history of Calgary Public

Library: *Calgary Public Library: Inspiring Life Stories.* She is currently researching and writing a guide to genealogical research in Alberta.

Holt, Faye Reineberg. Born in Stettler and raised on a farm, Faye lives in Calgary. She has authored 12 nonfiction books, a poetry chapbook, articles, interviews, short stories and (co-authored) a Travel Alberta book. An editor, Mount Royal writing instructor, former writer-in-residence, high school teacher and Glenbow history education co-ordinator, she has a blog entitled "Can't Quit Learning" and her website is www.wordsandhistory.ca.

Lawrence, Joan. Joan developed an interest in history at an early age thanks to hearing stories about her great-great grandfather, a carpenter and schoolteacher who came west by ox cart in 1875. She has written extensively about Calgary's human and natural history for Fort Calgary and other sites.

Marshall, Elizabeth. A former teacher, Elizabeth spent 14 years in the diplomatic corps. Her interest in the francophone history of Alberta developed while working in Edmonton for the Office of the Commissioner of Official Languages, in order to reply to the question, "Why do we have services in French in Alberta?"

Matheson, Shirlee Smith. Research, writing, and reading tours take Shirlee to schools, libraries, museums, and into the homes and hangars of aviation heroes whose stories are found in her 20 published books. Nonfiction books recall true tales of adventure and misadventure, while young adult novels appeal to readers of all ages. Shirlee was employed at the Aero Space Museum of Calgary for many years. Website: *www.ssmatheson.ca*

Pearson, Bob. Bob holds a Master's degree in Canadian History from the University of Calgary. He has been an interpreter at museums and historic sites in Alberta for more than twenty years. Bob is currently the Special Programming Coordinator at Heritage Park Historical Village.

Reeves, Kate. Originally from upstate New York, Kate Reeves has learned about Calgary by volunteering at Fort Calgary and Glenbow. Kate studied Heritage Resource Management and Museum Studies at the University of Calgary and is a past president of the local historical society. She is a certified local tour guide and has shared stories of her adopted city with locals as well as international visitors. She loves old buildings, especially churches, and has worked and volunteered at the McDougall Stoney Mission.

Lennard, Rob. Rob Lennard is the Historian and Director of Education & Outreach at the Historic Bow Valley Ranche at Fish Creek Provincial Park. He has written two historical fiction books: *The Amazing Alberta Time Travel Adventures of Wild Roping Roxy and Family Day Ray,* released in 2005 to celebrate the 100th anniversary of the province followed by the First Nation themed sequel entitled *The Amazing Time Travel Adventures of the Iron Crow Brothers and Bree Saint Marie.* Rob received both the Alberta Centennial Medal and Heritage Awareness Award for writing his centennial book and the sequel was voted one of the finest First Nation themed books in Canada for 2013-2014.

Romer Segal, Agi. Agi has worked with the Jewish Historical Society of Southern Alberta for over 20 years and currently serves as the archivist. She has also taught Jewish Studies in numerous settings and has translated Yiddish and Hebrew texts into English.

Walker, Valerie. Valerie enjoyed writing the chapter, *For Whom the Bell Tolls.* She is the author of two historical time-travel novels for juveniles, and five books about the adventures of *Hedley the Hedgehog* for kids 5-8 yrs old. Her latest book, *Looks Can Kill,* is her first Young Adult book.